Running for Office

Running for Office
The Strategies, Techniques, and Messages
Modern Political Candidates Need to Win Elections

BY
RONALD A. FAUCHEUX

M. Evans
Lanham • New York • Boulder • Toronto • Oxford

Published by M. Evans
An imprint of The Rowman & Littlefield Publishing Group, Inc.
4501 Forbes Boulevard, Suite 200, Lanham, Maryland 20706

Distributed by NATIONAL BOOK NETWORK

www.campaignline.com

ISBN 13: 978-1-590-77010-8

Printed in the United States of America

To
Joe, Jimmy, Mike, Ralph, Tom, Carl, Emily, Tony, Karla,
Roy, David, Joe Jr., Burt, Ruth, Chuck, Dick, Sharon, Al,
Leon, Lila, Fay, Lindsay, Rene, Lawree, Norma Jane,
Sandra, Mark, Jerry, Donald, Moon, Charlie, Nick, John,
Rusty, Harry – along with so many others who helped make
my first run a winner – and my parents,
who allowed me to run much of that first campaign out of
their dining room, living room, kitchen, guest bedroom and
garage.

Contents

★ Introduction

From an early age, I wanted to run for office. I started working on campaigns to learn the political process when I was in high school and managed my first congressional campaign the summer after I graduated from college. Within days of graduating from law school, I was off and running for the House of Representatives in Louisiana. In fact, I had to wait to get the results of my bar exam (thank God I passed it) before I could print my campaign literature.

After eight years as a legislator and two years as a state cabinet official, I left government service (voluntarily, I should add) and went into campaign consulting full time. In 1993, I became editor and publisher of *Campaigns & Elections* magazine, where I indulged my endless fascination with political campaigning by observing day-to-day changes in the process and then sharing new insights with up-and-coming candidates and campaign pros through hundreds of political training seminars and workshops.

This volume is an attempt to bring together insights into the incomparable process of running for office from my own experiences as a candidate and as a campaign consultant working with nearly a hundred candidates, together with my observations in more recent years of thousands of other candidates for a variety of offices – all brave souls who have had the guts to take the biggest plunge of all.

Nothing Like It

There's nothing quite like running for office. It's an unforgettable experience that many of those who do it would rather forget. That's because only about one in three political candidates ever win. But when it works and ends in victory, it's exhilarating; like nothing else on Earth. Noted one wag, flushed with the jubilation of an election night victory party: "If God invented anything better, he kept it for himself!"

Deciding to run is an easy equation for some, a logical next step. Occasionally, circumstances create candidacies. But for most newcomers and challengers, the decision can be complex and anguishing.

Even though it's easy to get caught up in the ego trip of being the center of attention, the intense personal commitment required of candidates is a matter that demands reflection and sober assessment. Candidacy brings high ups and low downs – every day. In fact, every hour. At two o'clock, you can feel like The Master of the Universe. By three o'clock, you're looking for Dr. Kevorkian's phone number.

The instability and uncertainty of campaigns, even the carefully planned ones, and the extraordinary mix of emotions tangled within them, strain the candidate, often making him or her feel like a piece of meat for everybody to cut up and chew.

Once you make the decision to run, it can be a relief. It may even be the most enjoyable moment of the entire campaign, matched only by the elation of victory. Those first few days when you tell yourself, "Yes, I can do it! Yes, I'm gonna do it!" are remarkably fanciful. But once the novelty wears off and the slugfest begins, feelings shift. It begins to seem as though a sword is hanging over your head, dangling on a thin thread, just waiting for any loon with a printing press or a fax machine to clip it, and your career, in one fell snip. Just ask Bill Clinton how he felt when he heard that Gennifer Flowers was calling a press conference. Or how George W. Bush felt a few days before the tight 2000 election when the story of an old drunken driving offense was about to break.

Making it through a strategically tricky race is like walking across a mine field. You may have lucked out here, but watch out! They may get you over there. When things are going well, you feel very, very well. When things turn a little sour, you feel very, very sour. The pendulum swings wider for candidates than it does for lesser mortals.

Political campaigns provide a unique view of society, revealing a cross section you cannot see anywhere else. They bring out the best and worst in people. When it's the best, it's touching; when it's the worst, it's excruciating. You haven't lived until a young child hands you his or her weekly allowance of quarters, nickels, and pennies to help your campaign. You haven't lived – and may not want to – until you find out that your second cousin has been caught passing out leaflets for the opposition because he thinks you're a loser and wants a favor from the winner.

New World

A scene in "The Wizard of Oz" has a young Dorothy confiding her suspicions to her little dog about being magically taken from a simple place called home to an inscrutable, more vivid new world. "Toto," she says, understating her fears, "I have a feeling we're not in Kansas anymore."

The same can be said about how political campaigning across the globe has changed into a new world of politics that is filled, like Oz, with inscrutable opportunity – and danger.

Technology and regulation have driven the biggest changes. Fax machines, satellites, PCs, desktop publishing, digital video editing, voter lists on CD-ROM, mass video duplication, cell phones, DVDs, Web sites, database management, e-mail, 24-hour cable news channels and phone bank predictive dialers have sped up the pace of politics and increased the costs. Enactment of campaign finance regulations – disclosure, contribution limits, public financing – plus liberalized absentee voting and vote-by-mail, combined with the effects of technology, have produced more expensive, professional campaigns.

These transformations have given us a new communications era, reflecting the pressures of media sound bites as well as the implications of new, commonly shared theories of voting and campaign strategy-making.

Throughout the 1980s, information emerged as the power tool of campaigning, be it about policy matters, legislative records or candidate characteristics. And with it, going into the 1990s, the new concept of message politics was born.

Political consultants now accept the notion that every campaign positions itself by conveying a message – which is the rationale they give to voters to persuade them to cast

12

their ballots one way versus another.

This concept emerged from the simple idea that the voting decision is a *choice.* Voters don't elect the best man or woman for the job but, instead, only pick between the available alternatives on the ballot on that day for that specific office. To make such a choice, it follows that voters focus on the differences – rather than the similarities – between candidates.

Contrast, therefore, became the centerpiece of message, and contrast necessarily meant some measure of attack. This, together with the ready retrieval of opposition research – often computerized and online – and an increasingly fractured media marketplace, gave rise to an explosion of negative advertising.

Surveys show that many good people are declining to run for office because they are repelled by the negativity, the scrutiny and the expense of the game.

Political campaigns have always brought out the best and worst in people. They offer participants a cross-section glimpse of society that is both penetrating and unique. They demand much, usually too much. By nature of the process, they yield more losers than winners. They are messy, confusing and ephemeral, and occasionally silly, mindless and ferocious, but they provide the pivot upon which our democracy turns. Without them, free government for, by and of the people could not exist.

Political competition, like war, is not for the squeamish or thin-skinned. It is hard and bloody.

Career advancement in politics demands resolve and boundless determination. The best political candidates are tough operators, able to throw as many punches as they take. But when they take the spotlight, whether it's in a race for school board or president of the United States, they should always remember, as Edmund Burke once observed, that they "sit on a conspicuous stage" and the whole world marks their demeanor.

In modern politics, running for office demands *preparation* above all else. And that's what this book is about.

★ Chapter 1

The Decision to Run

Serious questions you need to answer before you take the plunge

Running for office is a career milestone that can change the lives of many people. Too much is demanded of candidates and their families for them to take such a plunge lightly. Sudden flashes of egomania and shallow ambition may produce candidacies, but the decision to run requires more careful thought and deeper reflection. That's true whether it's your first time out or whether you're an officeholder who is looking to take a step up. In making the decision, there are 10 tough questions you should—no, make that *must*—answer:

1. Do I want the job?

Too often, candidates run just to be running, simply to get into public life, without much regard for the job itself. When this is the motivation, it usually shows. Once the press and the voters begin to sense a candidate's lack of interest in the job, it becomes increasingly difficult to be taken seriously.

Many public offices are not for everyone. A middle-aged business executive who enjoys managing large organizations may love being mayor of a big city, but may hate serving in the state legislature. A young idealist who's motivated by strong issue commitment may find serving in Congress a dream come true, but may abhor being sheriff or clerk of court.

2. Do I know what I want to do with the job?

At the end of "The Candidate," young Bill McKay (played by Robert Redford), having just been elected to the

U.S. Senate after a storybook come-from-behind finish, looks up in puzzlement and asks his campaign guru, "What do we do now?"

Unfortunately, many candidates run without a clue as to what they want to do with the job. A good example was Ted Kennedy's unsuccessful bid to capture the 1980 Democratic presidential nomination. Sure, Kennedy wanted it. But because he hadn't decided why he wanted it, his early days on the hustings were disastrous. His poor performance in the celebrated CBS interview conducted by family friend Roger Mudd, when Kennedy couldn't give a coherent argument as to why he wanted to be president, sharpened the point.

Many candidates want the job. Too many don't know what they want *to do* with it.

3. Can I take the time?

The naive believe they can simultaneously run for office and keep their jobs and businesses going at full speed. They don't understand that few things in life are as all-consuming as politics.

Unless it's a lopsided contest or one for a low-level office in a tiny district, campaigning takes time. A lot of time. Usually, more time than you have. There's always something else you should be doing: one more hand to shake, phone call to make, dollar to raise, news article to read, thank you letter to write or strategy meeting to attend. If you think you can run in a tough, competitive election and be a part-time candidate, think again.

Be prepared to live, breathe, eat and sleep your campaign. Or be prepared to lose.

4. Is this the right time?

Right person. Right office. Wrong time. The classic example was Hubert Humphrey. He mounted a spirited campaign for president in 1960, but that was John Kennedy's time. In 1964, fate catapulted Lyndon Johnson to the party's top spot on the ticket, relegating Humphrey to second banana. When he finally did win his party's nomination for president in 1968, it happened to be a ghastly year for Democrats—war, urban unrest, a crisis in confidence in national leadership. He barely missed.

By 1972, Humphrey's day had passed and the liberal wing of his party rejected him in favor of a new face, George McGovern. For Hubert Humphrey, the White House was not in the cards. Not because his party and his country didn't want him there, but because the time was never right.

Just like time passes some candidates by, others fall flat when they jump too soon. Al Gore's 1988 presidential nomination bid was a case in point, although the stature he gained from that campaign served him well four years later as Bill Clinton's vice presidential pick.

5. Can I take the name-calling, lies and gossip?

This may be the single biggest reason more good people don't run for office. No candidate is perfect. Everyone has flaws, has made mistakes and is susceptible to being embarrassed or misunderstood.

In politics, every crack of imperfection is magnified into a gaping canyon. Thanks to television, those cracks can be exploited by the opposition day in, day out—100 times a day—in living color, in the living rooms of your family, friends and neighbors. Add to that an increasingly snoopy news media, where every piece of personal conduct is under the microscope of self-righteous analysis, and being a candidate starts looking less and less appealing.

Hence, the *Halloween Rule of Politics*: If you have a skeleton in your closet—even just a small bag of disconnected bones—expect it to jump out before election day, and count on it to look uglier than you ever imagined.

Even though some candidates escape the sledgehammer, don't bet on being so lucky. Always expect the worst in politics. You'll rarely be disappointed.

Remember: If the skeleton is too big and ugly, you may do well to pass on running at all. If you do run, make sure your business and personal affairs (unpaid taxes, unsettled lawsuits, hiring of illegal aliens, criminal investigations, etc.) are in order.

6. *Can I win?*

You need a sense of objectivity and good research to answer that question. Most candidates can buy the latter. But few are blessed with much of the former. Wannabees often exaggerate their chances because they don't understand political arithmetic or human nature.

There have been legions of hardware store owners, flower shop keepers, Little League coaches and car dealers who think, because they meet hundreds of friendly people during the course of their work that (a) these people add up to an electoral base and (b) all those smiling faces will actually vote to put them into public office. Not so. In large electorates, the number of people you know isn't even a blip on the screen.

Many prominent civic leaders are shocked to find out from a poll that they only have single-digit name recognition and are even more shocked when they learn that their share of the vote in a trial heat is marked with an asterisk signifying less than 1 percent. Candidates shouldn't run if they aren't running to win. Getting exposure for your law firm is fine, but adding useless noise to the clutter of politics is distracting to the democratic process.

Candidates also hate to admit that many of those nice people who tell them to their faces that they're with them are, in fact, liars.

Follow the *One-Third Rule*: Plan on one-third of the people you meet on the street who encourage you to run to actually vote for you, one-third not to give a damn one way or the other (some don't even vote in your constituency) and the final one-third to ultimately be against you.

Those are the people who tell you they're for you! Imagine the range of feelings in the many voters who don't say anything?

Don't let the bright lights of the political process go to your head when you're trying to make this serious decision with so many consequences for yourself and others.

7. *Can I afford to lose?*

Some people, because they've already lost elections, or

because of the circumstances of the race, may not be able to survive a loss with their careers intact. This is particularly important when it comes to money. If you figure the only way you can finance a campaign is largely with your own money or on your own borrowing power, make sure if you lose you still can afford to feed your family. Some candidates who throw caution to the wind are elected; others have their houses repossessed.

8. Can I afford to win?

This is a relevant question in those contests for public offices that will take you away from your job or your business without adequately compensating you for your time, expertise or lost wages.

Most lawyers at one time or another dream about being judges. But some lawyers, when faced with a decision as to a possible judicial candidacy, forfeit the shot because they can't afford to give up a $400,000-a-year law practice for a $120,000 judgeship. Many legislators who are responsible for large businesses, budding law practices, insurance agencies or full-time employment find it hard to take the time off to go to the state capitol several months out of each year.

Another factor to consider is the bite of the political bug. Victory usually stirs ambition to go farther up the career ladder. What begins as a part-time commitment to serve on a local school board may grow into a desire to run for county supervisor, then Congress, governor and even president.

Beware of the bite! The toxin it spreads has few antidotes.

9. Can I raise enough money?

Financing is another obstacle that keeps a lot of good people—particularly women and minorities—out of public office. For some, raising money can be an experience that falls somewhere between having a root canal and an enema. Most candidates hate it. They wake up each morning dreading that they have to bleed strangers and, even worse, friends and relatives, for cash.

If you're not a Rockefeller, or an unbeatable chairman of the House Ways and Means Committee with lobbyists begging for the chance to write you a PAC check, fundraising is a tough business. If you have no easy money sources, and you detest asking for money, think twice about running.

10. Can I do this to my family?

Politics is hard on families of candidates. While close family members share few of the ego pleasures of a candidacy, they suffer many of the slings and arrows that come with political combat.

Remember 1992 presidential candidate Ross Perot ranting about Republican dirty tricksters disrupting his daughter's wedding? Candidates and their families are subject to cruel jokes, gossip and innuendo. It's open season on the way they look, act, think, dress and talk. Everything they do is going to be ridiculed by some jerk somewhere.

The long hours of hard work and being away from home don't help either. Losing, after taking all that abuse, can rack otherwise well-adjusted, sane people with bitterness and deep emotional scars. In politics, there's pain with every gain.

Whether you have the temperament and skills for political life is a question only you and your close friends and advisers can answer. Most importantly, it is a question that needs an answer before you enter the fray. The excitement of running for office and winning is incomparable. But so is the depression of being in the wrong place at the wrong time and losing. Think about both possibilities, and get ready for anything.

★ Chapter 2

The First 25 Steps Every Smart Candidate Should Take

Putting together the nuts-and-bolts of a campaign – from scratch

Potential candidates for public office would often come up to me at campaign training seminars and say, "I understand there are a lot of things I have to do, from raising money to hiring consultants to building an organization. But where do I start? What are the first steps I must take?"

The "First 25 Steps" is an attempt to answer these questions, to give candidates a simple, practical, step-by-step game plan to develop a candidacy from scratch.

The 25 steps are in no magic sequence. Depending upon your situation, you may want or need to do step eight before step four, or step eighteen before step fourteen.

They are offered as a checklist of crucial things to do. And if you do them, carefully and thoughtfully, you will be ahead of most candidates today.

1 *Make a final, irrevocable decision to run.* Search your soul and consider the implications a candidacy may have on your life and career. Ask yourself the hard questions we discussed in Chapter 1. Until you're sure you're in the race for keeps, and make a firm commitment in mind and spirit, you will never get off the ground as a candidate.

If you're going to run, run. If not, stay home and let somebody else do it.

Determined, decisive candidates will run rings around the Hamlets who interminably ponder – without resolution – whether to get into an upcoming race.

Until you've made a final, firm decision to run, it will be difficult – maybe even impossible – to get friends and potential allies to make commitments.

2 *Determine the rationale for your candidacy.* Before you enlist professional political consultants, figure out on your own what you stand for and what you want to do with the job you're seeking. What are your reasons for running? What is your public mission? Why should you have the job? Until you can clearly verbalize your rationale for running in 25 words or less, you're not ready to take the plunge.

Your initial rationale is what you carry in your head, and what you talk about in one-on-one conversations before you go through the more formal process of actually developing a campaign message (as we'll do in Chapter 4). It is what you take to your consultants when they're working with you to help develop your campaign message and issue themes.

Ultimately, your actual campaign's message may be much the same as your initial rationale for running. If that's the case, it's a good thing. It means that your early instincts were on target. But it may not be. That's why it's important that the campaign message be developed one step at a time.

3 *Get your resume in order.* This must be done a long time before the campaign begins. In some cases, years before. If you're only a few credit-hours short of an academic degree, you may want to go back to school and get your diploma before you run. If you're going to run on a pro-education platform, you may want to get involved in a local school committee – and do it long before you become a candidate.

Having a good story to tell about one's own life is a big asset for a candidate for any office. Sen. John McCain's heroic years in a North Vietnamese prison camp, for example, was the kind of compelling personal story that gave his campaign added public interest and his candidacy added personal credibility.

Most candidates have not had the experience of being a prisoner of war. But plenty of candidates have good, though perhaps less dramatic, stories to tell nonetheless. Many contenders for every office – from town alderman to U.S. senator – have genuine life or career stories of overcoming odds, clearing barriers and winning personal struggles. Those stories may involve bravery in war or skill in sports, compassion in helping the disadvantaged or innovation in building a business.

Candidates with compelling, or at least interesting, stories to tell are candidates who have a better chance to attract attention, and earn instant respect. Political consultants love such candidates, because they are so easy to sell to the voters.

If you have such a story, don't be afraid to allow your campaign to use it. But if you don't have such a story, don't try to invent or fake one.

Fudging a biography is a big mistake. When the deception is discovered, it'll destroy your credibility. If you feel you must show achievements you don't yet have, go out and earn them before you offer yourself as a candidate for public office. Then, armed with the right stuff, display it with accuracy, humility and honesty.

Many otherwise good candidates have lost winnable elections because it was revealed that they had claimed to be a graduate of a college they had, in fact, only attended. Or that they were not even a member of a civic organization in which they claimed to be a leader. Or that they lacked the military decoration or the community service award they proudly purported to have won.

Good stories are very helpful, but not so crucial that you can't win without one. If you lack a compelling biography or a rich resume, find something else for your campaign to talk about.

In presenting your background in campaign literature and ads, honesty – and accuracy – is always the best policy.

4 *Prepare your family.* Demands of a campaign are severe, especially if the constituency is large and requires extensive travel. Make your family part of your decision to run. Explain the risks and hazards of political life and the consequences of both victory and defeat. Prepare them for the inevitable lies, rumors and gossip they're about to confront.

5 *Get your business affairs in order.* Owe any back taxes? Have any lawsuits pending? Own a business that needs your constant attention? Head off problems before they do you harm. It may take considerable time to get your business affairs in order. That's why it's important to act early.

However you earn a living, make sure you have the time for a campaign. Many lawyers, insurance agents, real estate agents and small business owners who run for office think that because they control their own schedules they can both campaign and manage a business at the same time. This is usually not possible. As a candidate, there is always something you could or should be doing. Campaigning consumes your mental capacity and physical energy, making it difficult to do other things. Running takes undivided attention.

To avoid business losses and costly interruptions, make personal arrangements far in advance. Develop a plan that gets you out of the office and frees up your schedule.

6 *Carefully check all applicable election laws and set up a legal compliance system – before you accept or spend one penny.* There are many legalities candidates and committees must obey. In most jurisdictions, candidates have to file timely campaign finance reports. In some, personal income disclosure statements are required. Every candidate must, at some point, officially file his or her candidacy with either a party committee, a clerk of court, the secretary of state or a combination of some or all of these entities. Make sure you know the deadlines and work back from them.

Missing a deadline can be embarrassing, and costly. If tardiness involves candidate qualification papers, it may knock you out of the race. In 1994, a frontrunning congressional candidate in Indiana failed to file her candidacy papers on time – despite warnings – and was disqualified from a race she probably would have won.

To make sure you're complying with the law on every front, you need two things: (a) a good lawyer who will take charge of all legal obligations and (b) a good CPA who will take charge of all financial reporting. Keep your legal counsel and accountant in close touch with your campaign manager and political consultants. Often, what seems like a narrow legal or compliance matter can blossom into a big, nasty political issue.

7 *Raise seed money.* You'll need funds to cover initial exploratory and preparatory expenses before the public campaign begins.

If you're not an incumbent public official with a ready war chest or quick fundraising capability, getting the start-up dollars may not be so easy – especially if you haven't made a final decision to run or if you're still keeping your candidacy under wraps. As a result, many candidates use their own money to "test the waters."

Taking the first steps toward a candidacy often involves polling, buying office supplies, renting mailing lists, printing materials, hiring staff, traveling and retaining consultants.

A candidate in a medium-sized state legislative district may need as much as $10,000 to $15,000 in "seed" money; a congressional contender may need three or four times that much; a gubernatorial aspirant could require $250,000 or more.

If you can't afford to seed the fields yourself, you'll have to go to close friends, relatives, business associates and political boosters – people you've known a long time. This may be done through one-on-one candidate solicitations or the establishment of an "exploratory" committee headed by supporters who do the asking.

8 *Get professional help.* No, we're not talking about psychiatric counseling; although, in some cases, that may not be such a bad idea. But every candidate, no

matter how brilliant or seasoned, needs outside advice that's based on objective understanding of the political landscape and broad experience in the technical aspects of modern campaigning.

There are three functions in campaigns that should be handled by professionals: (a) research, (b) communications and (c) strategy. They each require technical expertise that most candidates do not possess.

Research. Typically, the most important research function – public opinion surveying – is handled by a polling firm. When you hire a pollster, make sure you get a firm that has a solid track record in competitive political campaigns. Don't trust this function to an inexperienced graduate student or college professor who wants to use you as a guinea pig to break into the business.

In larger races, you will also need to hire issue and opposition research personnel. This research, together with survey data, provides the information on which to base your substantive messages.

Communications. Your media consultant serves as your advertising and public relations agency. Though capabilities vary, most good consultants provide strategy advice as well as produce and place ads. Some are highly experienced in politics and will assume the role of chief strategist.

Media consultants with limited *political* experience – such as a local advertising or PR agency that makes ads primarily for grocery stores and car dealers – should be limited to technical or creative tasks such as designing logos and signs, taping and editing TV spots, etc.

It's better to hire a media consultant with a strong political background. But if one is not available or affordable, and if you're forced to rely on people without campaign experience, make sure someone with a political background – such as a general consultant, pollster or campaign manager – supervises the ad production and directs concept, message and the writing of copy. Beware of smart-sounding commercial promoters who don't understand politics. They'll likely impress you with their creative talents and chic buzz words – but if they don't know politics, they're dangerous.

The communications function includes "paid" media (TV, radio, billboard, newspaper and Internet advertising) and "earned" media (press relations). In smaller races, media consultants may also serve as *de facto* press secretaries. In larger campaigns, a full-time press secretary should be employed.

Strategy. General consultants are often hired to serve as chief strategists, spinners and planners. They may be experienced pros who have advised campaigns across the nation – such as James Carville, Ed Rollins and Dick Morris – or they may be local operatives with deep knowledge of the local terrain. Availability and budget will determine who you hire and what role they will play.

In many races, the pollster, media consultant or even campaign manager will assume the strategy function, eliminating the need for a separate general consultant.

In addition to general consultants, pollsters and media consultants, specialized consultants may also be needed for:

• Fundraising (writing a plan, soliciting political action committees, organizing events, etc.).

• Direct mail (writing copy, designing the pieces, overseeing the print production process, quality control, coordinating postal regulations, handling the mail drop).

• Telephone contact (hiring professional phone centers to make persuasive calls, recruitment calls, voter ID calls and get-out-the-vote calls).

• Web sites (design and maintenance of your Internet presence).

• Database management (setting up the hardware and software needed to keep track of voters, volunteers, contributors and correspondence).

Remember this distinction: Consultants work for multiple clients and devote only a portion of their time to your campaign. They're paid fees, retainers or commissions. Full-time campaign staff members – salaried or volunteer – have only one campaign to focus on.

Key campaign staff functions that must be filled in larger campaigns include:

• *Campaign manager* – the person who runs the entire

campaign operation, implements strategy, oversees staff, coordinates consultants.

• *Volunteer program coordinators* – staffers paid or unpaid who organize door-to-door canvassing, phones, voter registration, absentee ballots, early voting efforts, postcard and letter writing, coffee parties, signs, rallies, get-out-the-vote operations, poll workers and election day legal teams.

• *Field staff and grassroots organization* – staffers who organize political support among groups and by regions, communities and localities throughout electorate.

• *Advance and travel coordination* – in large district, statewide and national races, there is a need for staffers to handle travel arrangements and to assist local supporters in sponsoring events upon the candidate's arrival.

• *Database management* – if the campaign is large enough, you may need full-time staff to handle this function.

• *Press secretary* – a staffer who helps schedule media interviews, travels with the candidate, writes press releases, negotiates debate formats and rules, serves as the contact for reporters, sets up meetings with newspaper editorial boards, gives briefings and may even speak for the candidate under certain circumstances.

• *Communications director* – this staffer oversees the entire press/media/advertising operation and its coordination; also serves as "spin doctor" and "message enforcer."

• *Accounting/compliance/legal* – check writing, bank deposits, completing financial disclosure forms, filing legal documents, etc.

• *Coalition outreach* – works with supporters in established organizations that may include labor, teachers, business people, gun owners, bankers, home builders, insurance agents, national and local party committees, public employee associations, ethnic organizations, church assemblies, service clubs, women's groups, etc.

• *Fundraising* – a full-time finance director who manages the entire fundraising operation, including consultants, the candidate's solicitations, events and mass operations involving direct mail response mechanisms and Internet contribution fulfillment; coordinates with finance committee leadership.

See Chapter 10 on hiring consultants.

9 *Write a confidential autobiography for in-house use.* Before your media consultants can create ads and materials, they need to know your achievements, large and small. They need to know about your upbringing, ancestors and family life. They need to know your educational, civic and cultural background.

Many candidates are surprised when a good media consultant extracts a little particle of personal history – a sixth grade play, a volunteer project, an act of military bravery, a governmental accomplishment, an intimate family story, a funny comment from a relative – and turns it into the centerpiece of a powerful TV spot.

Your in-house "autobiography" should not be shown to anyone outside the inner circle, especially if it includes confidential or sensitive information.

Its length may range from two to 20 pages, depending upon the details and activities of your life.

In addition, it should be accompanied by an inventory of relevant family photos, films, tapes, plaques, diplomas, awards and other symbolic objects. If you don't want to let these keepsakes out of your sight – a lot of busy campaign consultants lose things – make copies of them so that your ad people know what's available and where to find it.

10 *Take a benchmark poll.* In most cases, you should take a poll before you even decide to run. Understanding the feasibility of your potential candidacy is critical to your "go" or "no go" decision. Depending upon your ability to fund early survey research, polls taken merely to "test the waters" of a possible candidacy will have a limited number of questions (thus holding down the cost) and, consequently, won't explore all the possible strategic scenarios. Once you're a "go" and need to finalize your actual plans, you should conduct a benchmark poll.

A benchmark poll will provide the road map for your

campaign strategy and message. It will test public opinion on candidates, politicians, institutions and issues. If properly designed, it will also test possible messages and slogans.

Only the smallest races, with the scarcest of resources, should attempt to live without a poll.

Most competitive campaigns that spend at least $50,000 take at least one professional poll.

11 *Develop a fundraising plan, put the fundraising team in place and start asking for money.* You can't get very far without money. In fact, you probably can't even get started without it. The finance plan and strategy need to be given as much attention as your political plan and strategy.

If the campaign needs to raise more than $250,000, consider bringing in a professional fundraising consultant. If the goal is a million or more, you have no choice. Even if your budget is under $250,000, the advice and help of an experienced consultant could make a big difference.

Many fundraising pros operate as part-time advisers. They'll help you coordinate your effort and, in some cases, make political action committee (PAC) contacts. They're paid fees and retainers. If they're directing a small-donor direct mail operation, they may receive some of their compensation in the form of commissions on printing, list rentals and mail processing.

Other fundraising pros serve as full-time salaried staffers and implement the finance plan on a day-to-day basis. They're usually called finance directors.

Larger campaigns need both.

Whether you have professionals helping or not, you'll also need volunteers – lots of friends and supporters who will ask for money on your behalf and who will sell tickets to your events. Your volunteer finance committee leadership will play the decisive role in building a person-to-person contributor network that will determine how close you come to meeting your funding goals. Select them with care. As the candidate, you need to make sure the volunteer leadership works hand-in-glove with your professional fundraising consultants.

Regardless of the size of your fundraising apparatus, in 99 percent of all campaigns, the candidate still has to ask for money personally. There's no getting around it. It takes plenty of direct candidate pleas, on the phone and in person, to get to the dollars you'll ultimately need. The lower the applicable legal contribution caps, the more time it takes.

Schedule candidate fundraising in chunks, full weeks and days at a gulp. Because begging for cash can be distasteful, it's easy to get sidetracked. If you go off somewhere and devote a full day, or even better, a full week or two, to the chore, without distraction, you'll get the job done.

See Chapters 7 and 8 on fundraising.

12 *Tour the terrain.* Before you announce, scout your constituency with the diligence of a map maker. Ride the roads and streets; check out the neighborhoods and businesses; learn where parks, playgrounds, churches, schools and shopping areas are located. Have someone drive you around for several days, or longer if necessary, with map and notebook in hand. Jot down your observations about the residents and landmarks. Give some flesh to polling and demographic data. When you've finished this exercise, you'll have a better visual sense of your constituency than anyone else in the world. That's a good start.

When I first ran for the state House, I was 24 years old and had spent a major part of the prior six-and-a-half years of my life out of town in college and law school. My parents lived in the district, but I knew very few people in the area.

My district – which had a population of about 40,000 people – was in the midst of rapid development, with new communities and subdivisions sprouting up every month.

To get to know the district's terrain, I got into a car with a friend of mine, and we literally drove up and down every street. It took us two Saturdays and two Sundays. While my friend drove, I had a clipboard on my lap and took notes on every block and neighborhood.

The tour gave me a chance to put a face on the numbers. It gave me a feel for the people and culture of every nook and cranny of my district.

After our four-day tour, I knew the entire area better than my opponent, a four-year incumbent.

Of course, if you're running for a statewide office, or even in a large congressional district, it is not likely you'll have the time to ride every street in your constituency. But you can still visit and observe *every* part of it, almost as a tourist would.

If you're a well-known public figure before you enter a race, you may not be able to tour your constituency in anonymity. At the start of Hillary Clinton's 2000 U.S. Senate run in New York, for example, she visited counties across the state as part of a "listening tour" – which served both as a publicity operation and a candidate learning endeavor.

Get to know your constituency, and the political geography, firsthand. Do it thoroughly, and do it early. Once the press of campaigning begins, you will no longer have the luxury of time to play tourist.

13 *Learn the issues.* Everybody has *opinions* on issues. Not many people have *knowledge* of issues. Most newcomers and challengers, especially those who do not yet hold public office, have serious information gaps compared with those who do. Before you go public with your candidacy, make sure you've researched the important policy issues and have a working knowledge of them.

Read news stories, magazine articles and research reports. Listen to, and tape, public affairs TV and radio programs. Think about how issues relate to average people and develop a series of anecdotes and simple statistics to explain them. If necessary, hire someone to help you put together issue papers that spell out (a) the facts and (b) your positions.

Good advice: After you decide you're running, but before going public, take a weekend vacation to a quiet place and bring with you a mountain of research material, clippings, books and articles. Study them like you're about to take a final exam. Get to know the factual context, with accompanying documentation, for each issue you must deal with and for each position you take.

Ignorance loses votes. Knowledge attracts them.

14

Hire personal staff. Most campaigns are large enough to require the hiring of a personal assistant to the candidate and a scheduler. These are two very important jobs.

1. The *personal assistant*'s job is to keep the candidate on track and on time. A key function is to serve as the candidate's driver. While many candidates will insist upon driving themselves, that's usually not very smart unless the constituency is a tiny one that requires little travel. Having a driver gives the candidate time to think and work in the car. It also saves time.

For example, the driver can drop off the candidate – to make an appointment or speech on time – and then look for a parking space. If the candidate is tired or has a drink or two at a party, the driver is a safety net against DWIs or embarrassing accidents. The driver can also bring campaign literature to public meetings and handle volunteer cards while the candidate is meeting-and-greeting.

Handling of volunteer cards is a function that should not be taken lightly. Every morning, when the candidate and personal assistant leave home for the day ahead, they should carry a stack of blank volunteer cards with them. During the day, every time someone offers to help the campaign the candidate or personal assistant should hand the volunteer a card to complete then and there. It's the job of the personal assistant to stand there while the card is being filled out and then to bring it to campaign headquarters.

This simple daily routine can build a large volunteer organization for almost any campaign.

See Appendix A for a suggested volunteer card format.

2. The *scheduler* is in charge of the campaign's most precious resource: the candidate's time. However much you pay this poor soul, it's not enough. While a good scheduler must juggle conflicting requests as a matter of course and take all the flak for saying no, often he or she will incur the wrath even of the person for whom he or she labors: the candidate.

Schedulers must work closely with personal assistants/drivers to keep everything on time and to avoid unproductive detours and dalliances.

Every meeting the candidate attends, whether it's a private one-on-one or a public speech, needs to be entered on the schedule with full information.

Candidates should never be sent into a meeting with anyone or any group without extensive information about what they want or what they can offer to the campaign. The daily schedule should answer these questions:

- *Who* is it you're meeting?
- *Why* are you meeting them?
- *When* must you be there, *when* does the meeting (or speech) start and *when* should you leave?
- *What* do you bring with you?
- *Where* are you meeting them?
- *How* do you get there?

The key to scheduling is specificity and precision. In answer to the *where* question, the answer is never just "the Holiday Inn." The schedule should include which Holiday Inn (in many places, there is more than one), the street address, directions on how to get there (if it's not commonly known) and the specific room.

See a suggested daily scheduling form in Appendix B.

15 *Set up an office.* The old-style storefront headquarters is – or, at least should be – a thing of the past. Modern campaigns are run from offices that are often out of public view.

In smaller campaigns, there is a temptation for candidates to use their homes or their business offices. Although this may save some money, it may not be a good idea. It's better to have a separate location from which to run your campaign; keep it apart from your personal and private business affairs as much as possible.

Although a campaign headquarters needs to be as clean and neat as possible, it doesn't have to be luxurious. It should have strong locks, a burglar alarm and open spaces to accommodate a myriad of volunteer projects as well as at least one private office for confidential meetings. It should house the campaign manager, scheduler, word processing staff and volunteer coordinators. If your inventory of signs, stickers and brochures is too bulky to store in your office, you may want to warehouse these items at a secure location nearby.

One issue that often crops up is whether a professional phone bank should be located in the campaign's main office. In most cases, the answer is no. Volunteer and paid operations do not easily co-exist under the same roof. That may also apply to fundraising, accounting and financial management. It's better to segregate these tasks from the loose, casual atmosphere that many volunteer-staffed operations acquire.

Remember: If you have confidential things to do (i.e., raise and count money, meet with powerful politicos, discuss sensitive decisions) don't do them in front of a lot of people. Consider the need for confidentiality when setting up your campaign office.

16 *Find a campaign manager.* This can be a difficult position to fill. It's a tough job that requires endless hours and total commitment. The candidate has to believe in the manager, and the manager has to believe in the candidate.

Campaign managers usually come in one of three types: (a) professionals who go from one election to another, (b) amateurs who are so good at it that they become professionals and (c) amateurs who have other careers and take on the job to help a friend or to further a cause.

Although any type will do if it's the right person, here are a few cautions: If you hire an out-of-state pro, make sure he or she is willing to make the effort to get to know the local political terrain. If you bring on an amateur, make sure that person either (a) knows what he or she is doing from day one or (b) knows that he or she doesn't know what to do but is open-minded about learning.

If an uninitiated campaign manager is given a role that is limited to only management and administration, leaving strategic and political decisions to others, that's OK.

But a little knowledge in a manager may be more dangerous than none at all. Amateurs who realize they're not crack political operatives will often eagerly learn from, and wisely defer to, those who are. Amateurs who lack varied campaign experience, but who nonetheless think they're another Lee Atwater or Larry O'Brien, can wreak havoc.

If your campaign manager is inexperienced, make sure his or her role is clearly defined to avoid unnecessary interference with your professional consultant team.

17 *Set up a strategy inner circle.* This should be a tight-knit group with a minimum of three or four people and a maximum of seven or eight people. This group would normally include the candidate plus the pollster, media consultant, general consultant (if there is one), campaign manager and a few other trusted advisers. It should encompass a variety of viewpoints and, when possible, at least one person who is not on the campaign payroll, preferably a seasoned politician with extensive campaign and governmental experience. This group should meet regularly (perhaps weekly) in addition to special meetings. Overall strategy and planning should be discussed, debated and decided at these sessions.

At least one member of this inner circle needs be kept on call on a 24/7 basis, as an emergency crisis management contact. This person would make himself or herself available by phone for quick advice and on-the-spot decisions when time pressures make it impossible to assemble the entire group. A crisis management contact protocol needs to be set up in advance so the candidate and/or the personal assistant can reach the on-duty adviser in an instant.

Oftentimes, something will come up (an unexpected press inquiry, a surprise attack, a major news story) that was not anticipated or discussed at the most recent strategy meeting. Consequently, candidates are forced to make judgments in a matter of minutes on critical matters without benefit of advice or reflection. Having a trusted adviser who understands the campaign's strategic goals within immediate reach by cell phone can provide the candidate with a quick and helpful sounding board.

Candidates need to be – and feel – in control. They need to maintain cool in every crisis. Knowing that help and advice is always a quick call away can be calming and reassuring in situations that could otherwise spin out of control.

In addition, the candidate and campaign staff need to know how and where to reach all members of the strategy inner circle for special meetings and conference calls when there is enough time to rally them together.

18 *Develop your campaign message.* Every campaign needs a public rationale, a compelling reason voters should vote your way. That's your message – and it's largely based on personal and issue distinctions between yourself and your opponent. Your message will frame the central choice you present to voters; it will position your candidacy relative to the opposition.

Candidates must internalize their campaign messages, feel comfortable with them and understand how to communicate them to voters and the news media.

Your professional consultant team and staff will play vital roles in crafting your campaign message.

For a step-by-step explanation of this process, refer to Chapter 4.

19 *Write a campaign plan.* If you have a consultant team and professional campaign staff, they should handle this chore for you. But as the candidate you must set the parameters and provide the basic information.

Every campaign plan should include the following:

(a) S*trategy memo.* It should deal with message positioning and sequence, timing and intensity, mobilization and persuasion considerations. This can be done in a page or two for small races and maybe three to five pages in larger ones.

See Chapter 3 for a full explanation of strategic elements that need to be encompassed.

(b) *Message memo.* It should explain your campaign message and related issue points along with an illustrative "message box." See Chapter 4.

(c) *Campaign budget.* This budget should be in two parts:

a line item "laundry list" of *how much* money you will spend by category and a timeline indicating *when* you will spend what. See Chapter 6.

It's important to know when you will need money so you can structure a realistic fundraising plan.

(d) *Fundraising plan.* How will you go about identifying and cultivating money sources in a comprehensive way? See Chapters 7 and 8.

(e) *Organizational chart.* Your chart should be as simple and realistic as possible and it should include all the professional and volunteer tasks necessary to run the campaign.

The first time I did such a chart in a campaign, I devised a massive paper bureaucracy that could have been used to win a world war. It had hundreds of boxes, jobs, functions, divisions, bureaus – and an impressive assortment of titles. The problem was that there were only five people to do everything! The next time I did an organizational chart, it was much simpler and more practical.

Your organizational chart should include:
• Professional consultants and their functions;
• Strategy inner circle;
• Campaign manager;
• Personal staff (scheduling, correspondence, personal assistant);
• Press staff (press secretary and/or communications director in campaigns large enough to be able to afford such personnel);
• Headquarters administration (office manager, campaign director, executive assistant, database management, material inventory and distribution, clerical);
• Field coordinators (who will organize counties, wards, precincts, neighborhoods);
• Volunteer recruitment and activities (i.e., volunteer coordinator, coordinators of each activity such as door-to-door canvassing, phone trees, postcard writing, sign placement, stuffing envelopes, election day workers, etc.);
• Coalition partners (coordinating campaign operations with party committees and advocacy groups supporting your candidacy);

• Regional campaign operations and offices (in constituencies large enough to justify such a structure).

(f) *Paid media plan.* This section describes what advertising tools your campaign will employ, how and when. Will you use television ads? Radio ads? Newspaper ads? Billboards? The Internet?

The media plan should also include a section on targeting. It should tie together the issue points you develop as part of your message memo together with budgeted activities to fire these targeted message bullets (through direct mail, phone canvasses, radio ads, cable programs, Web sites, etc.).

See Chapter 11.

(g) *Earned media plan.* This section discusses how you will go about seeking press coverage for your campaign and what strategies and messages you will employ through the news media. It should also discuss newspaper endorsements and proactive press events that can be coordinated with paid ad efforts. For example, you may want to combine regional TV news, radio talk show and newspaper interviews along with a bus caravan that's been advanced and reinforced by paid radio and newspaper ads.

20 *Establish a graphic "look."* Early on, it is important to select a consistent graphic theme with colors, type fonts, photos, layout and design. Failure to do so will delay printing of campaign letterhead, envelopes, cards, brochures, signs, buttons, banners and stickers.

In most cases, designing the "look" of the campaign will be the first task of your media consultant. It's also an early indication as to whether you and your media advisers are on the same wavelength.

Campaign graphics, on balance, should be clean, bold, simple and readable. Anything too cute or complicated should be avoided. In most cases, a simple dark (blue, green, black or red) background with white reverse type, upper and lower case, fairly tightly kerned, is adequate.

Getting great photographs of the candidate is critical. Don't skimp. Hire – or, make sure your media consultant hires – a professional photographer who understands political image making and lighting. Often, lighting is the difference between mediocre and excellent shots. Invest in a make-up stylist, someone who can get rid of circles under your eyes and facial blemishes.

Also, make sure your photographer shoots enough film – hundreds and hundreds of exposures if necessary. Don't let the photographer tell you he or she "got it" after a few camera clicks; make the photographer keep going so that your media consultant has a wide selection from which to choose.

If you don't want your pictures to look like something you'd see on a driver's license, take the time and spend the money to do it right.

In most campaigns, you need five basic shots. See Chapter 14 for a full explanation.

Make sure you get your photos done before the start of a busy campaign schedule. You want to look relaxed and well-rested, not harried and exhausted.

If you need to lose weight, change your hair style, get new eyeglasses or shave off facial hair, do it as early as possible, *before* the photos are taken.

21 *Determine your pre-announcement timetable.* Most candidacies are timed around four distinct periods. Understanding these phases in advance is important because it provides the candidate with guideposts that impact how you are to act in public, what to say and when.

You should attach specific dates to these phases and plan your personal contact schedule and campaign timeline around them.

(a) *Pre-decision phase:* This is the period during which the candidate ponders a candidacy. It is usually conducted in private and involves few people. It ends when the candidate makes a final decision to run.

(b) *Private preparatory phase:* This period begins after a "go" decision is made. It is limited to low-key, non-public preparatory activity. Usually during this period, the candidate is not ready to tell anyone outside of the inner circle that a decision to run has been made.

(c) *Public preparatory phase:* In politics, you can only keep something quiet for so long. At a certain point, usually sooner rather than later, word gets out and the prospective candidacy becomes public. During this period, the candidate openly acknowledges a likely candidacy though has yet to formally announce or file. Full-force planning is conducted during this period.

(d) *Post-announcement phase*: Once you formally announce your candidacy, it's open season for the press to ask you any question and for debates with your opponents. After your announcement, you will be expected to have positions on most issues and to be able to justify your stands. Do not announce until you are ready to "go public."

22 *Prepare "The Speech" and "The Book."* Every candidate needs an all-purpose speech that outlines your message and views on issues; it must be adjustable to differing audiences and situations.

In most campaigns below national or statewide levels, you rarely – if ever – are called upon to deliver formal addresses before massive audiences. Most political speeches are delivered before two dozen people in Holiday Inns.

Written speeches should be reserved for formal occasions and for speakers who are capable of presenting them. Ronald Reagan and Winston Churchill did better when speaking from a text. They were exceptional. Most candidates do better off-the-cuff, following a simple outline of major points.

A speech outline may include five to 10 bullet points that can be written on index cards or a few sheets of paper. Even if you're delivering a speech you know very well, having an outline is still helpful. It keeps you organized and makes sure you (a) cover all the important points and (b) don't repeat points you've already made.

You should prepare three speech outlines: one for a two-minute, one for a five-minute and one for a 20-minute speech. They will get you through most any occasion, including the opening of most multi-candidate forums and debates.

You should also assemble a number of inspirational quotes, funny stories, anecdotes and jokes that you can use to open, close and spice up public presentations.

Like everything else in a campaign, effective speech-making that moves voters requires plenty of preparation.

Woodrow Wilson was once asked how long it took him to prepare a 15-minute speech. He responded, "Two weeks." How long for a 30-minute speech? "One week." How about a two-hour speech? "I'm ready now," smiled the scholarly president.

It takes time to get your thoughts together in a coherent way. It takes time to figure out what goes in and what stays out. It takes time to get the timing right so that your speech is, as Winston Churchill advised, long enough to cover the subject but not so long that people lose interest.

You also want your speech to be uniquely yours, to have a theme that deals with the strengths and weaknesses of your candidacy. You want to believe what you say and you want to deliver it with passion and great enthusiasm.

The best way to improve your speaking ability is to tape one of your speeches. Then, after the event, in the privacy of your home, listen to every excruciating minute of the tape. Take notes on good things and bad. Just by listening, you will get a good sense of those areas that need work.

Once you complete your treatment of "The Speech," it's time to assemble your material and thoughts and one-liners, along with prepared answers to likely questions and supporting documentation, into "The Book." Type it all up in easy-to-read fonts (which may range from 14 point type to 72 point type, depending upon your eyesight). Punch three holes in each page and place the pages into a 1- or 2-inch ring binder.

Keep it with you all the time. Make sure there's a back-up copy at home or at the office.

Armed with "The Book," you're ready for anything, any time. If you're called upon to give impromptu remarks, or to answer questions, you always have something to consult – a security blanket. "The Book" is also an important resource for debates and forums.

By all means, watch over this document as if it's a million-dollar diamond: You don't need it falling into the hands of the press or the opposition.

23 *Get professional media and speech training.* There are many ways a candidate can learn about political campaigning. For starters, *Campaigns & Elections* magazine publishes "how to" articles in every issue on a variety of subjects (for more information, go to the Web at *www.campaignline.com*). A number of colleges and universities offer credit and non-credit programs in practical politics and campaign management.

There are hundreds of excellent books about presidential, gubernatorial and congressional campaigns that have been written by participants. Biographies of famous politicians are numerous, informative and inspirational. In addition, seminars are offered by political parties and associations that train candidates and staff in preferred techniques, tactics and strategies. These training sessions may be one, two or three day events, or more. The best ones pack a tremendous amount of useful information, practical tips and invaluable knowledge into a short time.

If you take advantage of free training programs offered by one of your party's local, state or national organizations, or a friendly advocacy group, you should consider supplementing them with nonpartisan training. Although partisan seminars give you a sense of what your side is doing and saying, nonpartisan programs – such as the ones sponsored by *Campaigns & Elections* and a number of universities – give you a more objective perspective, allowing you to see and hear what different sides are doing.

If your campaign entails making plenty of speeches and doing numerous TV, radio and print interviews, you should also hire a professional media trainer. No matter how good you are on your feet, or how many public appearances you've made in the past, you can always improve your approach.

Close elections are often won by candidates who win the nightly news sound bite game. Understanding the rules of the road, and the technical constraints of both electronic and print media, is critical. It's something every candidate must learn.

There are a number of wonderful media trainers in Washington, D.C.; Los Angeles; New York; and other major media markets. These pros have guided presidential candidates, governors, members of Congress and Fortune 500 executives. They're also rather pricey – charging $2,000 to $4,000 a day, or more.

There are also many competent, and less expensive, media trainers and speech coaches who operate in smaller local markets. Often, they include past or current talk-show hosts, news reporters and producers who have firsthand experience in how to handle the press and how to speak in effective, quotable sound bites.

24

Create personal contact pyramids – and start dialing. The first thing every candidate must do to get a campaign started is to pick up the phone and call people. These contacts should be undertaken according to a systematic plan, with appropriate follow-up and database management.

There are many strategically influential people you need to reach to get your candidacy off the ground. Some may be powerful politicians – or potential donors. Others may be interest group chiefs, media moguls, party leaders, business people, union officials, civic activists and local political operatives. Make a list of all of them and develop a time management plan on how and when you're going to make contact.

A key part of this effort is to database everyone – literally *everyone* – who may be helpful to your campaign. Make sure you develop a computerized contact system, similar to those used by real estate agents and stockbrokers to keep track of past and potential clients. Check out new software systems, off-the-shelf programs as well as those built for political campaigning. Pick one that suits your needs and your hardware.

For most campaigns where candidate fundraising is essential, you will need two contact pyramids, one for political contacts and the other for money solicitation.

In the top tier of each contact pyramid's peak, put the names of the three to 10 "Super VIPs" who will play the most critical roles. These people may have make-or-break power over your candidacy and need highest priority personal attention and follow-up. In some cases, you will need to talk to them during the "pre-decision phase" and in almost every case you will need to talk to them before your "public preparatory phase" begins.

In your *political* pyramid, Super VIPs may include major elected officials, possible candidates for the same spot, strategically positioned allies, party bosses and the most powerful leaders of business groups, trade associations, labor unions and/or issue advocacy organizations.

In your *fundraising* pyramid, Super VIPs will necessarily include your largest potential donors as well as possible fundraising leaders. In races where there are low legal limits on individual contributions (i.e., U.S. Senate, U.S. House, governors and state legislators in many states), making contact with a Super VIP who is an experienced fundraiser with the ability to quickly tap an established network of regular givers becomes critical.

Next, list 25-100 individuals in a "VIP" category. These contacts should be made during the "private preparatory phase." These may not be make-or-break people, but they are nonetheless very important to your campaign's success.

Everyone in these top two categories (Super VIP and VIP) requires one-on-one confidential meetings before the candidacy gets too far along.

Heavy-hitters have large egos. They need to be drenched with attention. Give it to them.

The third tier on each pyramid consists of "Priority Contacts." (In a small local race, this group may consist of only 100 people, or so; in a statewide or national campaign, it may exceed 1,000). Although Priority Contacts should usually be reached before the formal announcement, you may want to touch base with them by phone first and schedule personal meetings later.

This category includes second- and third-level political players who are often given short shrift by big-name pols.

They may be reached after the formal announcement – although in most circumstances earlier is better. People like to be in on the program from the start. A personal visit, or even a phone call, will do the trick.

Though this contact pyramid sets priorities by order of importance, every person you contact, whether in the top or bottom layer, should be made to feel special and should be treated like a big-deal insider.

Follow-up notes, thank you letters, invitations to campaign events and base-touching phone calls are all essential.

25 *Announce.* Official candidate declarations may be big news if you're a governor or U.S. senator announcing a presidential bid, but in most state and local campaigns they're usually formalities – and a good opportunity to get the press to run your picture and a biographical sketch.

However you make your announcement, make sure it fits your campaign strategy. Make sure your statement is in tune with your message and planned ads. Have your basic literature, signs, banners and stickers printed and ready for distribution. Have good photographs available for the press. Create a sense that the announcement marks the beginning, the starting gun, of intense activity.

Depending upon the size of the media market and the office you're running for, you may make your announcement simply through a press release or, you may do it in person at a press conference or at a campaign kick-off rally to add excitement and attract news coverage.

Most announcements at the local and district levels involve sending a photo with a two-page press release to media outlets – hoping they'll use them at some point in the next few weeks.

Cautionary note: Once you announce, you're fair game for public scrutiny, so make sure you're prepared to answer every possible question.

Happy trails!

★ Chapter 3

The Elements of Campaign Strategy

Just like military operations, political campaigns require the players to think strategically when making every move

Picture yourself playing chess, trying to checkmate your opponent. Only in this scenario, you're not at a chessboard but in a political campaign. Like the chess master, you need a game plan, a path to ultimate victory that anticipates the moves of your opposition. In politics, as in warfare of any kind, the master strategist is a realist who finds the path of least resistance to the ultimate goal of winning.

Some years ago, one of the all-time greats of the political consulting business, Matt Reese, convened a crew of campaign aficionados at his beachside home in Delaware. The purpose of the two-day poker-playing, gumbo-eating, cigar-chomping confab was to *define* political strategy. Reese wanted a way to explain this amorphous term – a term that means so much but is so poorly understood.

If you don't know what strategy is, he asked, how can you make it? How can you consider your full range of tactical options? How can you test your instincts and judgments against a standard of success?

In answer to Reese's queries, one was tempted to respond that strategy is like pornography: You can't define it, but you know it when you see it.

But that wasn't good enough for Reese, who had learned a thing or two about winning elections during his four decades in the campaign arena. He wanted more. Tell me, what is a *strategy*, he pressed, and tell me how it is different from a *tac-*

tic?

The best answer, I concluded, is that strategy is how you position yourself and allocate your resources to maximize your strengths and minimize your weaknesses. It is a *concept*. It is a way to win. A tactic, on the other hand, is a tool to implement strategy. It is *conduct*.

Roll Out

A political campaign should not be merely a series of events and activities haphazardly sequenced and arbitrarily timed. It should be rolled out with clear purpose as part of a logical plan.

Most candidates know they must have a coherent message, take polls, use modern database software, distribute literature, produce advertising, send out mail, make phone calls, identify and persuade swing voters, turn out supporters on election day – but figuring out *when* to do what, and to *what degree* and in *what order*, is something that often mystifies. Solving the strategy puzzle requires the ability to think strategically. And that's the key to victory.

This process is not unlike confronting a war among nations.

Political consultant Thomas "Doc" Sweitzer, in a *Campaigns & Elections* article, explained how the basic principles of military strategy apply to the political battlefield as well. They include: amassing strength against weakness; keeping focused on primary objectives; seizing the offensive and avoiding being placed on the defensive; simplicity of action; economizing use of force; maneuvering your way out of problems and over obstacles; unity of command and central decision-making; using surprise; and maintaining planning secrecy.

"The political world speaks in military tongues because war provides a useful model for political activity," elaborates Claremont McKenna College professor John J. Pitney Jr., who cites one of history's greatest military strategic wizards Carl von Clausewitz ("War is a clash between major interests, which is resolved by bloodshed – that is the only way in which it differs from other conflicts") as evidence for his thesis.

"Politics and war are remarkably similar systems," echoed Newt Gingrich as he commanded GOP battalions toward their widespread victory of 1994. "War is politics with blood; politics is war without blood."

No one can determine the right strategy for any campaign – political or military – without knowing the political context, the players, the issues, the terrain and the resources available. These factors make each campaign unique. One size does not fit all. Unfortunately, there are no magic wands and no certain results in this business.

Nonetheless, the strategy-making process in politics can be made less mystifying and more rational if you understand the elements of what a strategic battle plan should be.

Five Strategies

The first step in strategic thinking is understanding that every campaign needs a:

• *Positioning* strategy (which is, in effect, your campaign message).

• *Message sequence* strategy (the order in which you present the positive, comparative and negative components of your message).

• *Timing and intensity* strategy (when you do what).

• *Mobilization and persuasion* strategy (targeting voters to reach "persuadables" and "undecideds" vs. organizing and turning out "favorables").

To fully exploit situational advantages, or to overcome existing or anticipated obstacles, you may also need to maneuver through a range of *opportunity* strategies.

The following is presented as a menu of options that is, in effect, a checklist of strategic considerations that may be used and adapted in real-life campaign situations.

It is intended as a way to organize your strategic thinking for your next campaign, whether it's for a seat on your local water commission or for the presidency of the United States.

When presented with formulations such as these, many candidates and campaigners will be tempted to rigidly apply them, like a cookie cutter, to their own campaigns. Be very careful. Always remember that formulations of this type only serve as a general guide to developing your own strategies. Campaign strategy-making should never be a mechanical process where principles are applied without exception or revision.

I. Positioning Strategies

The essence of political strategy is to concentrate your greatest strength against the point of your opponent's greatest weakness. This is done through developing and delivering of messages that present voters with a choice based on candidate differences that are clear, believable and connected to reality.

Campaign messages may be based on:

(1) *Personal virtues and flaws* of the candidates, such as experience, competence, independence, integrity, compassion, stability, preparation;

(2) *Ideological and partisan differences* that may be based on notions of one candidate being liberal, conservative, moderate, radical, extreme, wishy-washy, inconsistent or pragmatic;

(3) *Situations* that may include big ideas such as change vs the status quo, the right track vs. wrong track, progress vs. stagnation; or

(4) A combination of any of the above.

At its essence, your campaign's message is what you say to voters to *position* your candidacy; it's the reasons you give voters why they should select you over the opposition. How and when you *communicate those messages* (the sequence, timing and intensity), and how and when you *mobilize your resources*, are the strategic components of every campaign, large and small.

For example, Bill Clinton's strategy in his 1996 re-election campaign was to *enhance* differences between himself and his Republican opposition on issues that benefited Democrats (Medicare, Medicaid, education, environment) and to *blur* differences on issues that benefited Republicans (crime, taxes, balanced budget, welfare reform, family values). By enhancing differences on favorable issues, he was playing to his natural strengths. He was, in effect, mobilizing his base. By blurring differences on less favorable issues, and by co-opting elements of Republican rhetoric, he was able to take many of these issues off the table, which made it easier for him to persuade swing voters to jump on his bandwagon.

The tactics Clinton used to implement this strategy included early "positioning" TV spots in targeted markets ("Gingrich and Dole on Medicare") and a series of speeches ("the era of big government is over"), legislative proposals (school uniforms, opposition to teenage smoking) and bill signings (welfare reform).

In the 2000 presidential election, polls showed that George W. Bush's strengths were related to his personality, leadership skills and family's values. Al Gore's strengths were related to policy issues and the incumbent administration's economic track record. It made sense for Bush to stress his strong points and to frame the election's choice around them. Gore's campaign, as a counterpoint, stressed his strong points, especially policy issues, as a way to frame the choice presented to the voters.

A criticism of Gore's campaign was that he didn't focus enough attention on the "track record" aspect of his message. Many strategists during – and especially after – the election speculated that Gore would have run a better race had he figured out a way to tie himself tighter to the improved national conditions that occurred during the Clinton-Gore administration ("You're better off than you were eight years ago") while keeping his distance from Clinton's personal behavior.

Framing the Choice

Messages may be used to de-emphasize candidate qualities and to highlight issues or, inversely, to de-emphasize issues and to highlight candidate qualities.

If your strength is ideological and your opponent's strength is personal, you may want to position your candidacy as a vehicle for *policy objectives* that overpower candidate virtues and flaws. The choice presented to the voters would then pivot on policy differences rather than on personality, character or credentials.

Another way to de-emphasize personality is to turn the election into a referendum "for" or "against" either (a) an overriding issue or (b) someone other than the candidates themselves.

Your campaign message draws the lines of distinction that separate you from the opposition. It frames a choice for voters.

How and when a campaign message is communicated to voters, as well as how and when coalitions are built and supporters are mobilized, depends upon the strategic formulations most appropriate to your circumstances. You then use the tactical tools of targeted direct contact (mail, phones, canvassing) and mass media (TV, radio, newspaper) to implement your game plan.

Selecting the right issues is both an art (a gut instinct for people and their opinions) and a science (polling, focus groups, targeting). It is also like music. You can either play big and loud over large themes like change vs. continuity, war vs. peace, the future vs. the past, or you can stress small, specific, concrete things such as school uniforms, anti-tobacco initiatives, computers in classrooms, elimination of the car tax.

The former is the James Carville "tuba" approach that was used successfully in Clinton's 1992 win. The latter is the Dick Morris "clarinet" approach that was used successfully in Clinton's 1996 re-election.

Candidate Inoculation

Inoculation is an important element of a positioning strategy; it is a way to blunt existing or potential weaknesses before they are allowed to kill your candidacy. Let's look at two examples:

• When Franklin D. Roosevelt was planning a political comeback after his polio affliction, he realized two things: (a) being a severely crippled paraplegic could be a major campaign liability and (b) an aristocratic candidate born into wealth and privilege could have trouble winning the trust of the masses. So during the years before his re-entry into elective politics, FDR developed a persona as a man of action, a strong, bold leader for change and a friend of poor, forgotten people. When opponents attacked him for "moving the country too fast," and when the rich criticized him for "betraying their class," it played right into his hands. His strengths were positioned in such a way that they also overcame his potential weaknesses.

• Clinton used inoculation strategies before his 1992 presidential race. To get around the "philanderer" image of a man who treated women as sex objects – a potentially lethal charge for a Democrat in the "Year of the Woman" – he took strong stands on women's issues and appealed to feminist groups.

To get around the liberal image that stuck to Democratic nominees George McGovern, Walter Mondale and Michael Dukakis, Clinton distanced himself from liberal orthodoxy – without offending most liberals – by supporting a "middle-class tax cut," endorsing capital punishment and taking indirect jabs at Jesse Jackson (a symbol of Democratic liberalism).

To get around being a "small-state governor," Clinton labored assiduously for years to develop an image as being a "national leader" (chair of the Democratic Leadership Council and the National Governor's Association) and cultivated California – the nation's largest state – into, in effect, his adopted home state.

Contrast these successful examples of inoculation strategies implemented years before their candidacies with Bob Dole's 1996 presidential campaign in which his age was a major liability. Unlike FDR and Clinton, Dole did not construct a persona and philosophy, through word and deed, over a long period of time, that negated this disadvantage. In short, he failed to inoculate.

II. Message Sequence Strategies

1. Ignore the Opposition
Open positive ➤ *remain positive to the close*

In this strategy scenario, you never attack the opposition nor do you respond to the opposition's attacks.

This strategy is often used by candidates with massive leads and large resource advantages – especially by strong incumbents against weak challengers.

The risk is if the opposition attacks. Unanswered attacks may be harmful, especially if they are credible and adequately exposed through mass media or extensive grassroots networking. In some cases, though, the frontrunner is so far ahead that the loss of a few points – say, going from 80 percent down to 70 or 75 percent – doesn't matter much.

This strategy option is based on the proverbial advice that you should "never dignify your enemies by mentioning their names." But modern campaigners understand the inherent risks of this strategy. Consequently, this approach is rarely used in highly competitive races.

2. Classic

Start positive and do not initiate an unprovoked attack against your opposition ➤ *respond to opposition attacks; may require going negative/comparative against opposition depending upon opposition attacks and effectiveness of your response* ➤ *end positive*

Consider using this strategy formulation if (a) polls show that you can win the race based upon a positive message because of inherent ideological, party or demographic advantages and (b) you do not have an abundance of usable ammunition to throw at the opposition. In effect, you lack an easily deliverable, low-risk "knock out" punch.

At various times you may pursue this strategy either on single or double message tracks – meaning how many types of messages (positive, negative/comparative/responsive) you convey simultaneously.

"Single message track" refers to using your communications tools to convey only one type of message (be it positive or negative/comparative/responsive) at a time.

"Dual message track" refers to a two-level message strategy in which both a positive and a negative/comparative/responsive campaign is waged simultaneously. A dual track is generally used to provide "cover" for the negative onslaught. When executed properly, it can reinforce your positive credibility while you're attempting to drive up your opposition's negatives.

When used, it's best to tie the two tracks together with a common theme (integrity vs. dishonesty, experience vs. inexperience, mainstream vs. extreme, in touch vs. out of touch, change vs. status quo, etc.). To pursue a multiple-track approach without framing the messages within a thematic context may confuse voters and diffuse the power of your arguments. Tight message focus is always critical.

This formulation is used by many campaigns.

3. Aggressive
Open positive ➤ *go negative before the opposition does* ➤ *respond to opposition attacks as necessary* ➤ *close either single track positive or dual track positive and negative/comparative*

You open positive to lay a foundation for the negative/comparative messages to come, and you attack your opposition before your opposition attacks you. You close on a positive note.

This strategy may be pursued at times on a dual-message track.

4. Frontal Assault
Open negative/comparative ➤ *then go positive and respond to opposition on a dual track* ➤ *close either single track positive or dual track positive and negative/comparative*

Use this strategy to draw deep lines between your candidacy and the opposition from the start. The idea is to "take out" the opposition at the beginning and then to build up your own candidacy after the opposition is weakened. You can achieve this strategic goal with both positive and negative message tracks that are designed to reinforce each aspect of the message by tying them together with a common theme.

This strategy option may be pursued using single or dual message tracks at various times along the way. It may also be used to "nip in the bud" the candidacy of a largely unknown rival before he or she has a chance to develop credibility or a base.

5. Relentless Attack
Open and maintain negative/comparative ➤ *introduce a dual track along the way with some positives at various times after opening* ➤ *close dual track positive and negative/comparative*

Use this strategy to draw deep lines between your candidacy and the opposition from the start. The idea is to "take out" the opposition first and then to build up your own candidacy after the opposition is weakened. You can close with positives and negatives simultaneously to reinforce both messages and to tie them together in a common theme.

III. Timing and Intensity Strategies

1. The Tortoise
Start slow ➤ *steadily build all the way*
While the opposition (the "hare") may be rapidly depleting resources and taking risks, you simply move slowly but surely along the path of least resistance that's timed to crescendo on election day without any periods of intense activity.

This could be a good strategy for well-positioned underdogs (i.e., they have inherent personal, ideological or strategic advantages) with limited money but with a lot more time to campaign.

2. Bookend
Open big and loud ➤ *then, a slow steady build* ➤ *close big and loud*
This formulation is often used by candidates with low name recognition and limited resources – although it does require the ability to fund a big opening.

The initial "bang" is used to attract attention and build credibility. Because resources are limited and the initial pace cannot be sustained, the activity level is lowered after the opening then stepped up again at the end to close with another "bang."

Important timing considerations: How long can you sustain the big and loud opening? One week? One month? How long can you coast between big bangs? The answer depends on available resources (money, volunteers, endorsements, issues, time).

In a one-year campaign, the middle "maintenance" period may last as long as 10 months; in a six-month campaign, five months.

In high-profile races, for example, free media can be used to sustain "maintenance" periods. In small district races, candidate door-to-door canvassing, signs and inexpensive literature drops can sustain the campaign during these times.

The "big and loud" close may take on the characteristics of a "blitzkrieg" – a lightning strike of activity that brings to bear all your resources and utilizes all your weapons in a quick, efficient, all-encompassing movement. Such a blitz may incorporate the "machine gun attack" formulation (see below).

3. Pearl Harbor

Open very quietly, causing your opposition to underestimate your strength and to misread your intentions ➤ *close big and loud*

This strategy is based on the power of surprise. It is the classic sneak attack. Catch your opponent asleep and then drop all your bombs at the end when it's too late for the opposition to mobilize and respond in a timely fashion.

The big gamble is whether you can cram the bulk of your persuasive effort and support mobilization into a short "close" period that may be as short as one week (in low profile races) or several weeks (in higher profile races).

This may be used most effectively in elections (a) where the opposition starts as the clear favorite (usually an incumbent who has grown out of touch and lazy) and (b) when your opposition, if given the benefit of extended planning and execution time, would be able to mount a successful counter-offensive.

In effect, it's a "one shot" gambit with little room for error. It often requires deployment of a blitzkrieg-type of attack.

4. Hold Your Fire

Slow, steady build ➤ *big and loud close*

A variation of the Tortoise, but with a big close. This strategy is designed to deploy resources at the moment of maximum efficiency and effectiveness: "Hold your fire until you see the whites of their eyes!"

The Tortoise spreads out its resources more evenly; Hold

Your Fire reserves more of its resources until the close.

This strategy was used to some extent by Republican National Chairman Haley Barbour in the 1996 congressional races. There was much controversy over whether the strategy worked. Some thought the Republicans had allowed Democratic attacks to last too long without strong countervailing measures. In the end, the results were mixed: While the GOP lost the White House, it did maintain control of Congress – which was the object of the strategy.

IV. Persuasion and Mobilization Strategies

1. Traditional Formulation
Create/reinforce base ➤ *identify undecideds/opposition leaners* ➤ *persuade undecideds/opposition to your side* ➤ *turn out supporters*

This approach fits most campaigns because it assumes that (a) you either have a base or can create one and (b) your base is not big enough on its own to win the race.

It is predicated upon the need to find "persuadable" or "swing" voters – those who are initially either undecided or leaning toward the opposition but subject to being swayed by your campaign's persuasive message. Once voters are brought into the fold through persuasion, they are added to the favorable voter pool that you reinforce and try to turn out on election day.

Supporters should be ranked by their strength of commitment ("hard" to "soft") and by their propensity to vote on election day ("likely" to "unlikely"). Get-out-the-vote resources should be concentrated on "hard" supporters who are "unlikely" to turn out without an extra push. The fewest resources should by expended on "soft" supporters who are "likely" to vote anyway.

2. Base Strategy
Reinforce base ➤ *then turn it out*

Usually for frontrunners, incumbents in good shape, plurality elections (where you win by getting the most votes regardless of whether it's a majority) or low turnout primaries and general elections. This is predicated upon having a base that's big enough to win on its own without adding "swing" voters.

3. The Marion Barry

Reinforce base ➤ *enlarge base* ➤ *then turn it out*

Question: How do you win an unwinnable election?

Answer: Make sure the electorate that votes on election day is unrepresentative (and more favorable to your side) of the electorate as a whole.

Use this strategy when (a) your base is not quite big enough to win without winning over opposition leaners and undecideds and (b) your prospects at winning over many opposition leaners and undecideds are slim to none.

Your base can be enlarged by two means: (a) voter registration and/or (b) election day turnout skewing.

To be successful, this strategy depends heavily upon tactical proficiency (i.e., the ability to stimulate and mobilize a high turnout of favorable voters relative to unfavorable ones).

This strategy was named for Washington, D.C., Mayor Marion Barry, who used it to make a spectacular comeback in 1994 after scandalous legal troubles nearly ended his electoral career.

V. Opportunity Strategies

1. Setting a Trap

Set up an attack by unleashing one aspect of it and withholding certain other information ➤ *opponent responds* ➤ *unload additional information (close the trap)*

For example: In a televised debate, each candidate can ask the other a question. Candidate A asks Candidate B his position on developing the state's tourism industry, knowing that Candidate B, as a former member of the state's tuorism commission, had missed 80 percent of the commission's meetings during his tenure. The trap was set by raising the tourism issue. Candidate B falls into it by discussing the issue without disclosing his poor attendance record. Candidate A springs the trap when he reveals the facts about Candidate B's dismal record.

2. Pincer Maneuver

Get opposition into a position they cannot escape without suffering losses

The objective is to surround your opponent, to deprive him or her of a safe way out.

An illustration of this strategic principle was 1997 Virginia gubernatorial candidate Jim Gilmore's proposal to repeal the state's high personal property taxes on cars and trucks. In making the proposal a centerpiece of his campaign's message, Republican Gilmore put his opponent, Democrat Don Beyer, into a strategic box. Advocating a big tax cut of any type was at odds with Beyer's central theme that the state needed to put more resources – i.e., money – into the state's educational system. In addition, the car tax cut presented Beyer with another hazard: As the owner of a well-known automobile dealership, his advocacy of a big car tax cut may have seemed particularly self-serving.

So, if Beyer opposed the car tax cut, he'd find himself on the wrong side of a very popular proposal; if he supported it, as some of his advisers had urged early on, he'd risk his credibility on other issues – such as education – that he had chosen to emphasize.

To deal with this tricky situation, Beyer at first was highly critical of Gilmore's tax cut. But then, he proposed a scaled down version of his own tax relief plan – a complicated $250 personal property tax credit. By so doing, Beyer got the worst of both worlds: He put himself in opposition to Gilmore's simple pledge to get rid of the car tax altogether and diluted his credibility on the issue by proposing a tax reduction that was (a) inconsistent with his earlier statements about policy priorities and (b) harder to explain than Gilmore's simple "No Car Tax" pledge. In the last days of the campaign, sensing that the car tax issue was killing his candidacy, Beyer changed tack: He blasted Gilmore's plan as a fraud and made scant mention of his own proposal.

In the end, Gilmore won the issue – and the election.

Pincer maneuvers may also be used in multi-candidate

races where contenders on the right and left simultaneously block the growth potential of a candidate in the middle. It may also be used in a two-way race where a middle-ground candidate moves toward a position that pushes his or her opponent toward a more extreme position (either on the far left or right) cutting the opponent off from competing for votes in the middle or on the other side.

In 2002, a variation on the pincer maneuver was used in the California gubernatorial primary. Gov. Gray Davis, the vulnerable Democratic incumbent, poured over $10 million into ads to influence the Republican nomination contest as part of an effort to weaken GOP primary frontrunner Richard Riordan, the independent-minded former mayor of Los Angeles deemed to be the strongest general election threat.

Davis attacked Riordan's record on abortion, claiming that the pro-choice Republican had an inconsistent history on the issue. In so doing, Davis put Riordan in a strategic box: By making abortion an issue during the GOP primary battle, he opened up Riordan to attacks from the right – pro-life conservatives were already suspicious of the left-leaning former L.A. mayor – and, at the same time, he set up Riordan for general election attacks from the left questioning the authenticity of his pro-choice position.

Riordan was stuck: If he reinforced his pro-choice credentials, he'd offend social conservative voters in the GOP primary; if he softened his pro-choice views, he'd risk losing existing support among pro-choice primary voters and would complicate his general elections prospects against Davis, a strong abortion rights supporter. To make matters worse, while the Davis media volley was hammering him full force, Riordan also took criticism from conservative primary foe Bill Simon for having supported many liberal Democrats over the years.

As a pragmatic centrist who had shunned party loyalty, Riordan took hits from both directions. He was put into a box from which he could not easily escape. Largely as a consequence of this pincer onslaught, Simon easily defeated Riordan for the Republican nomination, setting up the general election match the David campaign desired.

3. Poison Bait

Entice opponent to do something (go on TV, discuss an issue, spend money, etc.) that will self-inflict harm

A variation of Setting a Trap. In this scenario, you don't spring the trap yourself but entice your opponent to do it to himself/herself.

For example: Candidate A is a poor TV speaker. Candidate B does a TV spot attacking Candidate A for "not looking you in the eye and explaining what he stands for in this election." If Candidate A goes on TV, he's taking the bait and spends campaign money on a spot that may not be very effective.

4. Technological Advantage

Use an effective tactical tool the opposition isn't using and doesn't expect you to use

This may include your use of television ads, direct mail, door-to-door canvassing, telephone banks, sophisticated targeting, polling, opposition research or cable TV when your opposition fails to use them, thereby creating a technology gap in your favor.

5. Machine Gun Attack

Attack opponent on item #1 ➤ as opponent begins to respond to item #1, attack opponent on unrelated item #2 ➤ as opponent begins to respond to item #2, attack opponent on item #3

This is a classic attack technique designed to push your opposition into a defensive corner. Use when you have at least two or three separate attack arguments that address different weaknesses in your opposition and save the one that goes to the credibility of your opposition (the "knock out" punch) for the final blow. Of course, you need the right issues and candidates' differences to make this work.

6. Critical Mass

Overwhelm opposition with endorsements, money or physical presence and activity at a critical point

In this case, it's sheer volume that counts. If you can't beat your opponent with persuasion or mobilization based on issues and message differences, try crushing them with muscle, money or activity.

Occasionally, lazy frontrunners are outworked by underdogs who win because of sheer effort. Political machines have often won elections not because of fine-tuned messages, clever ads or creative use of issues – but because they had so much patronage and power to bring to bear that they engulfed the opposition.

Wall Street investor Jon Corzine used a money critical mass strategy to win a U.S. Senate seat from New Jersey in 2000. In that race, he poured over $60 million of his own funds into a campaign that swamped the outmatched campaign budgets of a former Democratic governor in the primary and a Republican member of the U. S. House in the general election. Corzine spent more money on his election day get-out-the-vote effort than many statewide candidates spend on their entire campaigns.

This strategy works best where resource imbalance is most extreme. Sometimes a spending advantage of two-to-one or three-to-one isn't enough. (For the record, Corzine outspent his primary opponent 12-to-1 and his general opponent 10-to-1). Because a steep imbalance is often hard to accomplish in a major election (Corzine's spending level was a record-breaker at that time), such an imbalance is often easier to pull off in smaller races.

Taking a lesson from Corzine's playbook – and checkbook – in 2001 billionaire Michael Bloomberg successfully used a money mass strategy to win the mayoralty of New York City in the wake of the September 11 terrorist attacks. In that race, Bloomberg spent $70 million, more than any nonpresidential campaign in American history had spent up to that time.

The Kennedys used critical mass effectively on behalf of JFK's races for Congress, the U.S. Senate and in the 1960 presidential primaries against an underfunded Hubert Humphrey.

Republicans often used this strategy successfully in special elections for Congress, although as party "soft money" and "issue ads" increased, the disparity in funding they once enjoyed has decreased, making a critical mass advantage more difficult to push. In a special election for the U.S. House in New York in 1997, beginning about two weeks before election day when the race was still fairly close, GOP committees dropped $800,000 on New York City TV time and $400,000 on direct mail. That was in addition to what the Republican candidate was already spending on his own. This massive soft money/party advocacy expenditure clinched it for Vito Fossella, the Republican who ultimately won a big 61 percent victory.

7. Firewall

Build solid pockets of political support that cannot be penetrated by the opposition under any circumstances

This strategy was used by Lee Atwater on behalf of George Bush's bid for the 1988 Republican presidential nomination. By building a *regional* firewall of impenetrable political support throughout the South, Atwater surmised correctly that regardless of the trouble Bush would have in Iowa, New Hampshire and other places, he would have the South to sustain him. Atwater, in effect, constructed a regional firewall for Bush.

In 1984, Walter Mondale's candidacy for the Democratic presidential nomination was based on an *organizational* firewall – regardless of what troubles he met along the primary route, he could always count on organized labor as the grassroots mainstay of his campaign in enough states to secure a large delegate base. Labor provided Mondale with a firewall constituency that his major rival, Sen. Gary Hart, could not penetrate regardless of how well he did in national polls or how much media momentum he gained.

9. Divide and Conquer

Enhance the strength of a third/minor candidate as a way to drain off votes from your major competition

The divide and conquer maneuver requires at least three candidates, whether it is a primary or a general election. A recent example was the 1997 special election for the U.S.

House in New Mexico. In that race, the Republicans captured a Democratic seat largely because the Green Party candidate siphoned off 17 percent of the votes, most of them at the expense of the Democratic nominee.

In multi-candidate races, a major candidate (the "beneficiary") can build up the strength of a third candidate by simply treating him or her like a major opponent.

★ Chapter 4

Crafting Your Campaign's Message

Every campaign conveys a message; here's how to make sure yours is the right one

Your campaign's message is a critical part of your strategy. It goes to the heart of how you reach out to voters and how you position your candidacy relative to the other contenders in your race.

In a true sense, *every* campaign conveys a message, whether it intends to or not. But not every campaign spends the time and effort necessary to craft a winning message. This chapter is about the process every campaign must go through to find the right message.

You can't talk politics anymore without talking about The Message. It has become the Holy Grail of electoral strategy, the sacred epistle of political communications. It is a term that stands for what every winning campaign must have. Your TV, radio, newspaper and direct mail must communicate it. Your speeches, sound bites and press interviews must reinforce it.

Political reporters and consultants fixate on the candidates' dueling messages. Smart campaign operatives will tell you it is essential that you not only have a message, but that you stick to it throughout the election.

So now you know you need a message. Your next question is probably: Well, what is it?

Your campaign message is your public rationale for running; it's the most compelling reasons voters should vote for you and not for the opposition. Simply put, it's what you communicate to the electorate that positions you and your candidacy relative to your opposition.

Frame the Choice

Effective messages set up a choice: Candidate A *versus* Candidate B. Unless it's a retention referendum, where voters get to vote an incumbent judge up or down, candidate elections are about choices between two or more people. When voters cast ballots for a candidate, they're not deciding whether that candidate is good or bad, popular or unpopular, perfect or flawed. They're choosing that candidate over another one. They're exercising an option, picking an alternative and doing it on the basis of what's available in that particular race at that particular time.

That's why differences between candidates are so important. Message-making, in effect, focuses on distinctions – not similarities – between combatants. It is little wonder that political campaigns have become so negative and comparative since political consultants of all parties and persuasions have embraced the theory of message politics that rests so heavily upon the notion of choice.

That's why you'll hear a voter pound his or her fist on a table and say, "I will never vote for Smith!" And then, six months later, he or she votes for Smith – not because Smith is so good but because the opposition is worse.

That's why a candidate who enters a campaign with a 55 percent negative rating is usually a dead duck; but if that candidate's opponent has a 60 percent negative rating, it's a different story.

Messages sit on the fault lines between candidates.

A campaign message can be expressed in a hundred different ways. It can be illustrated or symbolized using a variety of words and phrases. You can communicate it through slogans, signs and speeches; you can deliver it through electronic media or the printed word. But no matter how it is conveyed, it must be clear, consistent, understandable and relevant to the political choice at hand.

In terms of tactical presentation of a message, it must also be repetitive. You don't simply unveil a message, talk about it for a while, then discard it for another one. Messages need to be repeated over and over again. They need to be driven home before they can work.

Many candidates fear repetition. They feel compelled to experiment with new, untested themes at every stop. But this compulsion can lead to the blurring and complicating of basic campaign messages.

Richard Nixon, while president, was quoted as having given this advice to candidates: "Please don't try to please the press by saying something new all the time. Keep saying what works. Tom Dewey told me you have to tell people something at least four times before they remember it. We all have 'the' speech. Lincoln made the House Divided speech a hundred times before Cooper Union. Bryan made the Cross of Gold speech 259 times before the convention..."

You may be wondering, OK, I know I need a campaign message, but how do I create one? Where do I find it? Is there a Book of Messages I can buy? Is there a software program I can feed data into that'll spit one out? Unfortunately, it's not that easy. If it were, every campaign would be an automated competition where the result would always be certain.

Even though an effective campaign message can be described and dissected, developing it takes good instincts and solid judgment. That's where the science and the art of politics come together.

A campaign strategy includes a message and a means of delivering it (timing, intensity, sequence); a campaign plan details how and when you will implement the strategy and at what financial cost.

A campaign message usually incorporates *themes* (opportunity, change, fairness, leadership, integrity, the future, stability, continuation, etc.) that are reinforced by a series of *issue points* (proposals and viewpoints on education, crime, welfare, taxes, the environment, economic growth, health care, gun control, etc.) that can be used most effectively when directed toward specific voter groups.

Developing Your Message: Step-by-Step

The purpose of this chapter is to provide candidates a step-by-step guide to developing the right message. It's not a flawless formula, and it comes without a money back guarantee.

But it's a valuable exercise that every campaign should go through.

Since I introduced the step-by-step formulation in a 1994 article in *Campaigns & Elections*, I have been told that it has been used in many winning campaigns. Governors, members of Congress, state legislators and mayors have told me in recent years that they have used it in their victorious campaigns and found it to be a useful way to discipline their campaign's strategic thinking.

While our focus here is the development of your campaign's *central* message, your campaign may also need to develop *sub-message bullets* that are, in effect, specific appeals to targeted voter groups not inconsistent with the overall message. Sub-message bullets flow out of your targeting plan, which is based upon the coalition of voter groups you build.

Even if your message is obvious, you should test it before you marry it.

Here are the steps to follow in developing your campaign message:

Step 1: Do a demographic profile of the voters.

Get to know your constituency. Obtain numbers on voter group strength and remember that *population, voter registration* and *voter turnout* figures are three different things. Draw a simple statistical picture of the electorate by collecting data on partisanship, race, gender, age, employment, education, occupation, family status, home ownership, urban-rural, union membership, public employees, employment by industry, gun ownership, sexual orientation, religious groupings, special issue attachments and traditional "Hatfield vs. McCoy" rivalries.

After you get the numbers, drive around your district, city or state. Look at it. Get to know its communities, neighborhoods and people. This will put a human face on the numbers.

2. Do an attitudinal profile of the voters.

Take a hard look at voter attitudes in your constituency. The first step is to have an experienced pollster do a survey. A base, or benchmark, poll can give you an overall reading of the political landscape, demographically and ideologically. What issues matter? What public figures are liked and disliked? Is the nation, state or locality on the wrong or right track? What kind of candidates are they looking for and why?

This type of survey should probe possible messages by using a variety of question techniques. If done properly, it's like mining gold. It's amazing what unexpected gems will pop out of a poll with a well-structured questionnaire.

Step 3: Do a coalition profile of the voters you need to win the election.

Though nearly every voter thinks of himself or herself as an independent-minded individual, most of them vote according to discernible group patterns. You win elections by gathering enough support within enough groups to get more votes than your opponent. That's called coalition-building, a fundamental task of any political movement.

Because of the nature of the beast, candidates often want to run campaigns that appeal to nearly 100 percent of the electorate. In so doing, they convey messages that are mush. By trying to appeal to everybody, they end up not appealing to anybody.

You see, if your campaign is based on a message that is so broad that it appeals to far more voters than you will ever get, or ever need, the message will end up being shallow, generic, banal and generally useless. Such messages are losing messages. That's because, while you're dealing in soft irrelevancies, one of your opponents will start picking off groups of voters with harder, direct appeals.

Developing a coalition profile is simply determining what voter groups you will stitch together to win. The tricky part is that each group you will need – be they Republican white males, Democratic white women, African-American homeowners, rural gun owners, public employee union members – has a different agenda.

For example, pro-choice Democratic women under 40 who are members of public employee unions may often vote the same way in presidential elections as do retired African-American men over 65, but they have different perspectives and disagree on certain issues. If you need to get a high percentage from both groups to win your election, you need to identify the common denominators that bring them together. You need to develop messages that appeal to both.

To develop a coalition profile, divide the electorate into politically useful categories that are simple to understand and meaningful to your candidacy. Then, answer this central question: What is the right combination of voter groups that will get me to a majority (or, where applicable, a plurality) of the vote on election day?

Look to polling data, voter demographics and past election returns as guidance for determining the right combination you're seeking.

For example, if Candidate A is a liberal Democratic woman running for the state legislature against Candidate B, a conservative Republican male, and Candidate A's district (based on polling, past election results and turnout history) is split 24 percent Democratic women, 21 percent Democratic men, 20 percent Republican women, 19 percent Republican men, 8 percent Independent men and 8 percent Independent women, her coalition profile may look something like this:

Sample Coalition Profile			
Group	*The Group's Share of the Electorate*	*% of Group Candidate Needs*	*Cumulative Points*
Democratic Women	24%	84%	= 20.16
Democratic Men	21%	70%	= 14.70
Independent Women	8%	60%	= 4.80
Independent Men	8%	45%	= 3.60
Republican Women	20%	30%	= 6.00
Republican Men	12%	19%	= 2.28
Cumulative Percentage Points			= 51.54
			(enough to win)

Coalition-building entails finding ways to bring together voter groups that often exhibit dissimilar political behavior. To get her magic 51 percent of the vote, Candidate A will have to build a coalition consisting largely of Democrats and women; to do that, she will need a message that primarily appeals to her Democratic base and secondarily attracts a sizable portion of women Republicans and Independents. Issues such as abortion, school vouchers and capital punishment pose opportunities and dangers in this case since they are usually salient among voters she has targeted.

If a survey of the district shows that 75 percent of the Democrats and 50 percent of the Republican women are pro-choice on abortion, then Candidate A may want to stress that issue. On the other hand, if Candidate A opposes the death penalty and Candidate B supports it, and 55 percent of Democratic women and 80 percent of Republican women agree with Candidate B, this is clearly a perilous issue Candidate A should avoid. If Candidate B is smart, he will use it to drive a wedge between the groups Candidate A needs to cluster together in her winning coalition.

In building an ideal coalition profile, there may be more than one path to victory. If there is, test a few scenarios and go with the one that makes the most sense. Take the path of least resistance.

Let us jump ahead for a moment and take note of something very important: Your coalition profile is the basis of your campaign's targeting plan that will identify which voters you will need to mobilize, which voters you will need to persuade and which voters you will need to ignore.

Your coalition profile together with your targeting plan will provide a basis for developing issue points, which are specific pitches that *are not inconsistent* with your campaign message but that can be used to move key voter groups by stressing specific matters that are the most pertinent to them.

For example, a Republican candidate for the state legislature who is running against an unpopular, 30-year Democratic incumbent may develop a central campaign message that stresses the idea of change ("After 30 Years, It's

Time for a Fresh Approach and New Leadership"). But in addition to running on a theme of change, this challenger may also be able to develop more specific issue points that can be targeted to specific groups (an anti-government regulation pitch to small business people; an anti-gun control pitch to gun owners; a pro-property tax cut pitch to home owners, etc.).

When targeting issue points to select voter groups, it's important to stress that they should never be in conflict with your campaign's central message. Rather, your issue points should reinforce and give substance and documentation to your message.

In the example we just used, the GOP challenger's targeted issue points do not weaken or contradict in any way this candidate's message of "change." In fact, they help flesh out the change message with relevant specifics.

In summary, your coalition profile provides direction and form to your entire message-making process. It also provides a basis for your targeting and media plans, your campaign budget, your persuasion and mobilization strategy and the use of segmented issue points.

Step 4: Inventory your strengths as a candidate.

Make a list of your strengths as a candidate and as a prospective public official – strengths that may potentially appeal to voters. Be objective. Ask friends and advisers, confidentially if necessary, and get an honest reading. Also use survey research to measure, when possible.

Always keep in mind the politics of your electorate, the temper of the times, voter partisanship and ideology, current hot issues, recent events that have shaped pertinent public perceptions and the demographics of your constituency.

Strengths may be *personal* or *political*.

• Personal strengths include such things as a reputation for honesty and integrity, a background of experience, coalition-building success, leadership skills, personal strength, relevant training and a record of accomplishment.

• Political strengths would include having popular positions on issues and being on the right side of situational matters (change, continuity, etc.).

When considering political strengths that relate to specific policy issues, it should be remembered that every issue has at least two sides. On almost any policy matter, some voters will like your position and some will dislike it. The balance on one particular issue in your constituency may be 60-40 percent in your favor, and on another issue it may be 55-45 percent against you, but in both cases there are some voters in your corner. This means, your position on most issues can be both a strategic strength (among like-minded voters) and a weakness (among voters who disgaree) at the same time.

In most cases, an issue is not politicially advantageous in terms of message-making if the majority of public sentiment is opposed to your viewpoint. However, an issue stance that is shared by only a small minority of voters may still be a strength in terms of reaching and mobilizing that small targeted voter minority. In short, a relatively unpopular position may be a bigger weakness than it is a strength, but it may still be a strength at least among that segment of voters who stand with you on it.

In addition, though your position on an issue may not be popular, your courageous, straightforward handling of that position may have public appeal and that, in itself, may become part of a larger message that is based more on personal, as opposed to political, strengths.

Step 5: Inventory your weaknesses as a candidate.

Make a list of your weaknesses as a candidate and as a prospective public official. Again, be cruelly objective. Ask friends and advisers to contribute, confidentially if necessary. When doing this, also keep in mind the various factors that will likely influence public perceptions of your candidacy.

Personal weaknesses may include things like inexperience, a reputation for dishonesty, poor legislative attendance, inability to work with people, image of incompetency and being too old or too young.

Political weaknesses may include unpopular positions on issues, ties to a controversial politician or administration and being on the wrong side of a situational matter such as change vs. the status quo.

Step 6: Inventory the opposition's strengths and weaknesses.

Make lists of strengths and weaknesses for each of your opponents or likely opponents as you did for your candidacy. Although it may be somewhat unpleasant to objectively identify the opposition's strengths, the most fun you'll have in this whole exercise comes when you get to list their weaknesses.

Step 7: Draws lines of distinction between your strengths and the opposition's weaknesses.

Study all of the inventory lists carefully. Now, determine three things:

• *What "mirror opposite" strengths do I have that contrast directly with the weaknesses of my opposition?*

The strongest campaign messages rest on "mirror opposite" strengths you have that play against parallel opposition weaknesses. For example, if you have an unblemished reputation for honesty and your opponent is publicly under criminal investigation for bribery and racketeering, you have the perfect "mirror opposite" on integrity, honesty and trust issues.

In 1992, Clinton's message centered on change, a perfect pitch to use against an incumbent whose party had been in office for 12 years when voters were looking for something different. Also, Clinton's image as a "people person" played well against Bush's image as an out-of-touch elitist, particularly when it was related to economic issues.

Contrast that to the effort to defeat Bush four years earlier. In 1988, voters did not want dramatic change. The economy was still doing well and many voters were afraid to change what they perceived to be successful Reagan-Bush economic and foreign policies. As a result, Dukakis could not make change stick as a message, a big problem for the out party. Because Dukakis was considered more of a technocrat than a populist, he also had trouble playing against Bush's personal weakness.

Something else to keep in mind: Often, a "mirror opposite" strength, although it sets up a good contrast with your opponent, is not big enough to become all or part of your central message, although it may still be a very effective attack argument.

A case in point: In 1992, polls showed that Dan Quayle was a drag on President Bush's ability to appeal to undecided voters and that Al Gore was an across-the-board asset for running mate Bill Clinton. This, of course, was a "mirror opposite" strength for Clinton. Although it was a very important issue that worked to Clinton's benefit, it was not appropriate as the central campaign message. Clinton would have looked foolish campaigning on the theme, "Elect me and you'll get a better vice president." Clearly, the distinctions that could be drawn on the "mirror opposite" economic change message were much more powerful and appropriate.

In the early Republican presidential primaries of 2000, frontrunner George W. Bush ran into stiffer competition from Arizona's Sen. John McCain than the Bush campaign had originally calculated. McCain's big New Hampshire win and rising poll ratings in the upcoming South Carolina primary forced the Bush campaign to rethink its message, which – to that point – had been a fuzzy combination of the candidate's personality, morality, leadership skills, accomplishments as governor of Texas plus his celebrated blend of "compassionate conservatism."

But to derail McCain, it was believed Bush would need a sharper message that drew a clearer distinction between himself and his major opponent at hand. So, to juxtapose their candidate's perceived strengths (leadership skills, executive ability, record of accomplishment as governor of Texas) against McCain's perceived weaknesses (a single-shooter who didn't work well with others; a legislator who gets great press coverage but passes few bills), the frontrunner unveiled a new slogan that was the byproduct of a new message: "George W. Bush: A Reformer Who Gets Results."

Bush's new slogan illustrated his new message, which positioned him as a reformer (to co-opt McCain), but also as someone who could get results through skillful, bipartisan leadership. Additionally, the new message represented an attempt by the Bush campaign to broaden the definition of the word "reform" beyond McCain's notion of campaign finance regulation (which had attracted so much media attention and editorial support) to include a wider range of policy matters involving taxes, Social Security, education and civil liability.

Bush's midcourse correction was late in coming and was executed in the glare of press skepticism, but it was ultimately successful; he went on to defeat McCain in the Super Tuesday primaries and, of course, to win an easy nomination in Philadelphia that year. The McCain threat had been disposed of, but it took a sharpened campaign message that concentrated on "mirror opposite" strengths to help get it done.

• *What major "stand alone" strengths do I have that my opposition lacks?*

If you have no clear "mirror opposites," "stand alone" strengths become important as a substitute. They also form the basis of the positive side of your campaign.

An example of a "stand alone" strength would be if Candidate A has a great record of civic involvement (chaired charitable causes, volunteered for years in community service projects, etc.) while Candidate B has only a fair one. Even though this may not be a clean "mirror opposite" strength since Candidate B is not without some civic experience to point to, it's still a good "stand alone" strength that Candidate A can use to build a favorable case for his candidacy.

How do you know the difference between a "mirror

opposite" strength and a "stand alone" strength? Try this variation of the last example: if Candidate A has a great record of civic involvement and Candidate B has no record and was also caught lying about it, a "mirror opposite" strength exists for Candidate A – a clean kill by anyone's estimation.

    • *What "mirror opposite" or "stand alone" strengths does my opposition have, and what weaknesses do I have, that could become the basis of attacks against me?*

This is the flip side of itemizing your strengths. Example: Candidate A is running for the city council and is only 23 years old with no governmental or business experience. Candidate B is 40 years old with eight years of governmental and 10 years of business experience. In most elections, Candidate B would have two related "mirror opposite" strengths: age and experience.

Attacks against you, and attacks against your opponent, are not limited to "mirror opposite" strengths and weaknesses. You are subject to being attacked on any and all weak points you have, as is your opponent.

The difference between a candidate's "stand alone" weaknesses and his "mirror opposite" weaknesses from a public attack standpoint is that while "stand alone" weaknesses may make good attack material, they are probably not as effective as a campaign message as are those that have a "mirror opposite" effect. Nevertheless, they still may become part of the mosaic of attributes that buttress your message.

Be careful with your "stand alone" weaknesses, even minor ones. Your opponent may try to develop "stand alone" strengths into "mirror opposites" either through unanticipated events or by providing new information that may enlarge your weaknesses and magnify his or her strengths. Make sure you inoculate yourself before being attacked.

Step 8: Craft the message.

It's now time to bring all this information together. Focus

on the lines of distinction between your strengths and your opposition's weaknesses. Now, draft a message for your campaign.

Write down a sentence or short paragraph that summarizes the reason the voters should elect you, keeping in mind your strengths, the opposition's weaknesses and your need to inoculate against your own weaknesses. When you write this statement, keep in mind everything we have discussed up to this point: voter demographics, attitudes and the likely coalition of voter groups you will need to win. Also keep in mind the issue points that support your claims. When you're finished this exercise, you will have your first draft of a campaign message.

Examine the strength and simplicity of these two well known samples of effective campaign message-making. In 1984, the winning Republican presidential election message on behalf of President Ronald Reagan when he was running against former Vice President Walter Mondale was:

> *Things are better now than they were four years ago because of Ronald Reagan's leadership. His policies have improved the economy, reduced inflation, cut taxes, curbed the growth of government and strengthened the nation's military defenses. Let's not go back to Carter-Mondale.*

Reagan's re-election message answered the famous question he had posed during the 1976 campaign debate with President Carter: "Are you better off than you were four years ago?" In so doing, it tied four years of domestic and international change and improvement to Reagan's leadership skills as president and it linked Mondale to the "malaise" and uncertainties of the Carter years.

In 1992, the winning Democratic presidential election message on behalf of Bill Clinton when he was running against President George H. W. Bush was:

> *Bill Clinton will bring change and an improved economy. He understands average people and their need*

for new hope. Bush-Quayle doesn't. That is why he
will work for a middle-class tax cut, expanded oppor-
tunity for the disadvantaged (working women,
African-Americans, gays and the poor) and afford-
able health care for all.

Clinton's meesage focused on national discontent with
the status quo, especially as it related to the economy. It
framed the election as a choice over domestic issues and priorities and centered the voting decision on the need for populist change.

Your campaign message, like that of Clinton's in 1992
and Reagan's in 1984, should contain concise and specific
answers to these basic questions:

• Why do you want the job and what will you do with it?

• Why are you better than the opposition for this job at
this time?

• What public policy issues and situational matters support the need for your election?

Step 9: Draw a Message Box.

A good way to think about your campaign message, and
to illustrate it in a way that is both understandable and simple, is to create a Message Box.

A Message Box, in effect, breaks down your message into
four parts: what you will say about yourself; what you will
say about your opponent; what your opponent will say about
himself or herself; what your opponent will say about you.

By including both your positive and negative messages,
and those anticipated from your opponent, you provide
yourself with a full view as to how the message battle will
play out, both offensively and defensively.

The best way to explain a Message Box is to look at an
example of one that was used in a winning campaign.

In 1996, only one incumbent U.S. senator (Republican
Larry Pressler of South Dakota) was defeated for re-elec-
tion. He was beaten by at-large U. S. Rep. Tim Johnson, a
Democrat, in a tight contest. Karl Struble, a media consul-

tant and campaign strategist, explained in an article published in *Campaigns & Elections* magazine how he developed for the Johnson campaign a Message Box that was used as the basis for the advertising and communications effort on behalf of his client. It is an excellent model.

Here's what Struble's Message Box for Johnson's campaign looked like:

Challenger Tim Johnson's "Message Box" In U.S. Senate Campaign Against Incumbent Larry Pressler

Johnson on Johnson

Tim Johnson is different from most politicians. He's on our side. He's taken on the powerful to fight for the needs of average South Dakota families.

• *votes to protect Medicare*
• *fights for family farmers and water projects*
• *plan to hold down pharmaceutical costs*
• *raise minimum wage*
• *v/chip/cleaning up the Internet*

Johnson on Pressler

Larry Pressler has changed. He's "gone Washington" and sold out South Dakota families to promote policies that benefit the rich and powerful.

• *votes to cut Medicare, education, farm programs*
• *votes to give tax breaks to the rich and corporations*
• *junkets, first-class travel, abuse of office and campaign finances*

Pressler on Pressler

Larry Pressler is a common sense conservative. He is changing Washington to get government off the backs of South Dakota families and re-establishing traditional family values.

• *helped pass welfare reform*
• *pro-balanced budget amendment*
• *passed Telecom bill*

Pressler on Johnson

Tim Johnson is a liberal. He supports the tax and spend policies that are ruining our economy and permissive values that are destroying the American family.

• *votes against a balanced budget amendment, welfare reform and tax cuts*
• *abortion*

A Message Box illustrates both the positive and negative components of a campaign's message as well as the issue points that give substance to the message. In this example, Johnson's message was, in effect, a combination of "Johnson on Johnson" and "Johnson on Pressler":

> *Tim Johnson is different from most politicians. He's*
> *on our side. He's taken on the powerful to fight for the*
> *needs of average South Dakota families. That con-*
> *trasts with his opponent: Larry Pressler has changed.*
> *He's "gone Washington" and sold out South Dakota*
> *families to promote policies that benefit the rich and*
> *powerful.*

Johnson's campaign used this message as the rationale for his candidacy. This is the choice his campaign framed. This is how he presented the decision he hoped voters would see, and make, on election day.

But in addition to his message, the box includes a variety of *issue points* (i.e., votes to protect Medicare, fights for family farmers and water projects, plan to hold down pharmaceutical costs, etc.). These issue points served two purposes: first, they provided substantive documentation for the message itself; and second, they were tailor-made for targeted communications (sub-messages, if you will) to segmented voter groups.

For instance, based on this box, Johnson could send mailers to farmers about Pressler's votes to "cut farm programs"; he could send mailers to seniors about Pressler's votes, as he characterized them, to "cut Medicare"; he could send mailers to public school teachers and parents talking about Pressler's votes, as he argued, to "cut education." These issue points provided Johnson's campaign with the basis for a targeted direct contact strategy with both positive and negative components.

Step 10: Test your message.

If you can answer "yes" to each of the following questions, then the central campaign message you've now developed is probably on the right track:

Question 1: From a geographic, ethnic, partisan, social and demographic perspective, will this message appeal to the groups necessary for my winning coalition?

This is critical. If your message offends one or more of the voter groups you need to coalesce around your candidacy, it's a loser. A poll is the key to answering this question.

Question 2: Does this message zero-in on both your strengths and your opposition's weaknesses? Does it take full advantage of "mirror opposites," if you have any?

Go back through the lists you've made and recheck them.

Question 3: Does this message apply uniquely to you in this race (as opposed to being so generic that any other candidate could use the same message just as appropriately)?

Candidates who run on the basis of their general qualifications and experience when their opponents have comparable credentials are using a message that's so innocuous it doesn't grab.

Many candidates like soft, mushy messages because they fear harder ones will offend too many voters. But a message that tries to appeal to everyone, in most cases, ends up not appealing to anyone.

Campaign messages are about substance. Repeat: Campaign messages are about substance. They are about specific differences between candidates. They are not simply shallow slogans or superficial rhetoric.

After you come up with your message, try substituting your opponent's name for your name. If it applies to him or her as well or almost as well as it applies to your side, then it's probably too general and needs to be sharpened.

Question 4: Is the message big enough? Is it something that hits home with voters? Is it clear enough for them to understand?

Campaign strategist James Carville once advised *Campaigns & Elections* readers that elections are won on "big" issues and "big" messages, things such as war and peace, prosperity and depression, change versus the status quo, honest versus dishonest. He said, "Political campaigns are music and the tuba will beat the clarinet every time. You've got to play big and loud over big issues, big things."

The earlier example of the 1992 vice presidential candidates was a good illustration of a contrasting "mirror opposite" strength that helped Clinton but was not "big" enough by itself to serve as the central message. Economic change was.

Question 5: Are you a credible messenger for this message?

Many campaigns devise the right message but their standard-bearer has no credibility delivering it. When that happens, it's time to think about changing messages or getting out of the race. Often, right-message wrong-messenger candidates end up helping another candidate in the race who is in a better position to capitalize on public sentiment.

Question 6: Does the message help in some way to inoculate you on points where you are weak and subject to attack?

If Candidate A, who is running for sheriff, has no background in law enforcement, while Candidates B and C do, Candidate A may want to craft a message that attempts to turn his lack of experience into an asset.

In this case, for example, if the last two sheriffs both had strong law enforcement experience when they were first elected but were forced to leave office in disgrace because of scandal, perhaps Candidate A could develop a message around the theme: *We've had enough corrupt insiders running our sheriff's office. We need new leadership and an outsider perspective on how to run an honest department.*

It's a shot anyway.

Often inoculation can be done through the projection of vivid personal imagery. A very young candidate can wipe away a perception of being young-and-unprepared by demonstrating otherwise through mature carriage. A very old candidate can achieve a positive effect by projecting physical vigor and new, futuristic ideas.

Franklin D. Roosevelt, who was severely crippled by polio, was unable to take even one unassisted step when he ran for president in 1932. The biggest criticism of him was that he was moving too fast, that he was doing too much, that he should slow down and give the country a chance to catch its breath.

FDR proved that a firmly established image of political mobility could go a long way toward eliminating what could have been an image of physical immobility. Whether he could have done that in modern times with news photographers capturing his every move is another question. Nevertheless, Roosevelt was a master at the inoculation game and his career is a stunning example of how it can be played with success.

If you can answer these six questions with a certain "yes," then it is likely you have found a good message formulation. If you answered "no" to any of these questions, or have doubts, go back through all of the steps and do it over. Don't stop until you get it right.

If, after trying again and again, you still can't find the right message, you can always ask a professional campaign consultant or another objective person for help. Or, if you've already tried that option, you can reconsider whether you should be a candidate for *this* office in *this* election.

After all, if you can't convince yourself why you should win, how can you persuade the voters?

What Candidates Say to Voters

Candidates need to convey their messages in a way that is interesting and memorable. This may seem simple, but it's often hard for many candidates to grasp.

A great illustration of how this works in reality was a reported exchange that took place between Max Kennedy, son of the late Sen. Robert Kennedy, who was preparing a run for Congress in a Boston special election in 2001, and his consultant, Doug Hattaway. According to an article in *The New York Times Magazine* by Matt Bai, after the 36-year-old Kennedy did a listless run-through of a dry announcement speech draft that had been written for him, there was a feeling that something was missing.

Hattaway asked Kennedy, who had never run for office before, to think about *why* he was running, and then to express it:

> "What's the take-away message to the speech?" Hattaway wanted to know.
>
> "Huh?"
>
> "What do you want people to take away from it? When Mabel goes back outside and sees her neighbor on the street, she says, 'I saw Max Kennedy.' 'Oh, really? And what did he say?"
>
> Kennedy thought for a moment, standing uncomfortably at the lectern. "He's really a nice guy, and he cares about me. He'll work harder than anyone else."
>
> "But what's the take-away message?" Hattaway persisted.
>
> "That I'm a nice guy," Kennedy said again, exasperated. "And I care about health care, jobs, education, environment." These were the four pillars of the stump speech.
>
> "OK, but what will you *say*? What's the one thing that people will hear?"
>
> Max Kennedy shook his head and shrugged. He looked like a man on the verge of giving up. "I don't know," he sputtered. "Whatever it takes."
>
> – *The New York Times Magazine, July 15, 2001, "The Kennedy Who Quit" by Matt Bai*

Max was going to run as a Kennedy and a nice guy. But he didn't have anything to say that gave voters a reason as to why *this* Kennedy, *this* nice guy, was running in *this* election. In effect, he didn't have a message.

A few days after the disastrous run-through, Max Kennedy announced he wasn't running.

The point of this story is not to pick on a Kennedy. It is a story that is repeated thousands of times in every election by candidates for large and small offices across the nation, Kennedys and non-Kennedys, alike.

Campaign messages are more than merely saying you're a nice guy. (Your opponents may be seen as nice guys, too.) They're more than merely saying that you care about the issues that polling data tells you are the most important to voters. (Your opponents may say they care about the same issues, too.)

Campaign messages are about what *you* offer as a candidate. They are about how you tie your own, unique, personality and issue package together. They are about, in the end, why you're better than the opposition in *this* election for *this* office.

Message-making requires precise thinking and sharp contrasting. It requires threading the proverbial needle, getting your position just right – not too far left, not too far right, not too low and not too high.

Just as consultant Hattaway said, every speech needs a "take-away message" that voters will respond to and take with them.

Campaign messages provide the strategic positioning of your candidacy. Campaign speeches provide the poetry and personality of your candidacy.

A speech is one way, along with your campaign's advertisements, to *explain, dramatize* and *personalize* your message. It is a way to paint the right pictures, to ring the right bells, to push the right buttons.

If you don't have the right message, you won't deliver the right speech.

If you have the right message, then the next step is to find the right words, the right phrases, the right emotions and the right stories to illustrate it. And to do it in a way that fits your own style, enhancing your particular strengths and inoculating against your particular weaknesses.

Primary vs. General Election Messages

You may now ask: OK, now I know how to develop a message; but what if I have to run in a primary against one set of opponents and then in a general election against an entirely different opponent? How do I reconcile that?

Of course, if you're unopposed for your party's nomination, or are running in a nonpartisan race, against only one opponent, your message-making process will be much simpler than if you're running against more than one candidate in more than one contest.

For candidates running against a field of candidates, you need to, first, identify and include only your major opponents, those candidates that pose a potential threat to you. (Notice I said *potential* threat. That's because in some primaries, opponents who begin as unknown long shots eventually emerge as major contenders based on effective campaigning and strong candidate appeal. If in doubt, keep them in.)

When you inventory the strengths and weaknesses of your serious or potentially serious rivals, it's usually a good idea to treat them as one, as a single oppositional bloc, in terms of analyzing their collective and individual strengths and weaknesses. By so doing, you can draw "mirror opposite" and "stand alone" contrasts against the whole bloc, where appropriate, as well as against some of the individuals as well.

When developing a message to be used in a competitive primary, you must keep two things in mind: first, the need to win the primary; and second, the eventual battle in the general election.

Candidates who are fixated too early on the general election, and who ignore potential competition in a primary, oftentimes find they don't ever get to the general election.

A good example was the 2001 Republican primary for governor of New Jersey. In that race, GOP party leaders selected former U.S. Rep. Bob Franks, a moderate, as their candidate because they believed he'd be their strongest horse in the November face-off against the Democrats. The Franks campaign expected to have an easy time disposing of underdog primary opponent, Jersey City Mayor Bret Schundler, a social conservative who had stronger appeal to ideological true-believers. The Franks' people started their primary campaign in *general election* mode. But a few weeks before the primary, Schundler's grassroots, insurgent campaign gained combustion – and couldn't be stopped by a last-minute media blitz by Franks. On primary day, the underdog upset the frontrunner with 57 percent of the vote.

So, the point is: Take each race at a time. That's because

each race is different. The opposition is different, and the issues and contrasts between candidates are usually different.

When you're facing both a competitive primary and general election, your message-making process is necessarily complicated by having to fight two completely different battles. The best way to handle it is to craft your primary message first. Make sure it sets up the right contrasts and frames the right choice for you to win the nomination. But at the same time, avoid anything that would serve as a barrier to winning the general election. Also, for best results, include in your primary message certain themes that you can carry right on through to the general election to give your campaign an air of stability and consistency.

Then, in the general election, craft a new message that fits the changed circumstances. As such, it should attempt to carry forward themes from the primary (since you've already built up credibility for them) while at the same time drawing a contrast against your new opposition.

Each election has its own peculiar conditions, with its own dynamics and calculus. Your messages should reflect that, but they should also keep in mind that voters expect a sense of continuity about what candidates say.

 **Chapter 5**

Art of the Attack

How to go after your opponent – without having it blow up in your face

For a comparative or pure attack ad to be effective in a campaign, voters must view it as being fair. What's fair? In the context of partisan politics, with charges hurling back and forth, it's often hard to tell. But there are some rules of the road that campaigns can follow not only to make their ads appear to be fair but to make them, in fact, fair – and defensible – while still making them effective in terms of winning elections.

To work, attacks – as with most campaign messages – need to be:

1. *Believable.*

Even if it's true, it won't be effective if voters don't think it's true.

For example, when U.S. Rep. Rick Lazio closed his 2000 U.S. Senate campaign in New York by attacking opponent Hillary Clinton for being in cahoots with Middle East terrorist groups, it appeared to many voters as an "over the top" smear. Even among voters who had a strongly unfavorable opinion of the controversial first lady, the Lazio argument that she would somehow show support for international murderers was too much to believe. As a result, what was once a fairly close race ended in a 12-point defeat for Lazio on election day.

2. *Clear.*

Don't complicate it with unnecessary words or charges. Make sure you stay away from long, convoluted arguments that demand intense concentration to follow. The thrust of an attack should be susceptible to being summarized in a simple sentence.

3. *Logical.*

Don't undercut one claim with another, inconsistent one. Candidates are usually tempted to throw everything at the opposition, and end up making arguments that weaken one another. Political campaigns are not lawsuit petitions where you can make allegations in the alternative. In a campaign, you can't make one argument and then say, "Well, if you don't buy that, what about this?" Political attacks are an accumulation of impressions and information presented; they need a bottom line to cut.

4. *Documented.*

The information should be based on a legitimate public record. The documentation should be clearly presented in your ads so voters are assured they are rooted in legitimate fact.

5. *Timely delivered.*

Timing is everything in campaigns. Using your best material too early can ruin its ultimate impact. Dropping it too late may not give it a chance to penetrate, or percolate.

6. *Fully delivered.*

If you think you can print an attack flier, put it on people's front doors the night before the election and that will suffice – think again. If you're going to unleash an attack, make sure it gets out to all the voters you want to receive it. Consider a media mix that includes more than one medium.

Attacks usually invite counterattacks. So you want to make sure your original attack message has penetrated the electorate before the counterattack begins.

7. *Precisely accurate.*

Don't misrepresent the facts. Don't exaggerate them, either. Don't push a point beyond where you can easily justify it. For example, if your opponent voted to increase taxes 10 times and fees nine times, don't try to stretch those votes into a claim that he or she voted to raise taxes 19 times. Stick to the more conservative number (10) so you don't open yourself up for a cred-ibility-jarring counterattack.

8. *Relevant.*

Attacks should pertain to the issues at hand and to the office being sought. If they don't, they'll likely look like unfair mud-slinging. They can also invite press ridicule if they seem too far afield.

9. *In the right tone.*

Snarling, nasty, malicious is out. Reasonable, thoughtful, bal-anced is in. That's why comparative, as opposed to pure attack, ads are usually better. Political attacks are very delicate things. Treat them that way, with great care. Make sure each word and phrase conveys the right mix of authority, fairness, objectivity and energy needed to get your message across.

10. *Prepared for the comeback.*

Don't think for a second that you're going to be able to criti-cize your opponent – even if it's a reasonable, thoughtful, bal-anced criticism – without your opponent coming back at you. And expect the comeback to include a new attack, this time against you.

If possible, inoculate yourself against the expected counterat-tack before it is even made.

Moral of the story: Think through all the implications and possible responses before you pick a fight.

Just like there is an art to attack politics, there is also an art to counterattacks.

Counterattacking

All 10 rules of attack apply to counterattacks. But two addition-al rules apply:

1. *Counterattacks should not only answer the original attack they should also include a new attack against the attacker.*

The goal is to put, and keep, your opponent on the defensive. Attacks are meant to do that. Therefore, an effective counterattack will get you off the defensive and turn the tables on the attacker in a way that puts him or her on the defensive.

For example, if A attacks B for voting against programs for education, B answers the charge and then adds an attack against A for voting against tough crime penalties. "No wonder my opponent is misleading you about my record on education, he wants to get the focus off of his dismal record on crime."

2. Counterattacks should be made in kind.

If you are attacked with a TV spot, the response usually should also be with a TV spot. A TV attack should not be answered just on radio. Or by a flier drop.

The toughest call to make in this regard is if the attack came through the mail or phone calls. It's not always possible to respond in kind to mail or phone attacks, because you don't always know precisely where they went. Sometimes, you may be forced to counter mail or phone attacks through a multifaceted response that may involve a combination of mail and/or phones, as well as TV ads, radio ads and earned media.

★ Chapter 6

How Much Will It Cost?

A quick and simple guide to realistically budgeting your campaign

To develop a campaign budget, you have to start with a coldly realistic assessment of the money you will have available for your campaign war chest.

1. Determine how much money is available.

The first step in determining your funding potential is to take a sheet of paper. Divide it into three columns. Label column one Sources, label column two Minimum, label column three Goal.

Under sources, list all your potential fundraising sources, from Aunt Bessie to local home builders, from EMILY's List to gun owner groups, from labor union committees to personal loans from the candidate, from the captains of industry to small donor supporters. Make sure you include the amount of money you personally donate or loan to your own campaign. Of course, you need to make sure your sources and amounts are consistent with applicable state, federal and local campaign finance laws.

For each source, fill in the "minimum" contribution you know you will get and the "goal" (for maximum) you think you may be able to get and what you should ask for.

Example: Aunt Bessie, though not extremely wealthy, is fairly well off and has always considered you one of her favorites. You know she's good for at least $500 and think if you plead and beg (which before it's over you'll end up doing), you may be able to squeeze as much as $2,000 out of her in several increments. So, put $500 next to her name in the "minimum" column and $2,000 in the "goal" column.

Now, add up the "minimum" column. Take half of that number and that's what you can probably count on to raise from this list of sources. Don't be depressed if that figure is far short of your fundraising needs. If it looks like you're a winner, the numbers will increase. Also, if you run a well-organized finance operation, you can increase the results.

Remember too, that this is your initial source list. During a campaign, you will identify many new sources, particularly if you're well-organized and look like you have a chance at winning.

This exercise is a good way to force candidates into making a realistic analysis of how much money is out there. This is an essential first step to budgeting a campaign.

This is a critical part of the plan. It is always wise, and often depressing, to be honest with yourself when doing a budget. In politics, as in business, things usually cost more than you first think. Price increases, unanticipated problems, administrative overhead, crisis management, all of these things can easily make mincemeat of a campaign budget.

2. Pick a budgeting approach and stick to it.

There are a lot of different approaches to budgeting. Some consultants suggest you do high, medium and low budget scenarios, or ideal and barebones scenarios, depending on fundraising. You need to find the approach best geared to your needs. In any case, select one and use it throughout the campaign.

Perhaps a better suggestion is to do a single realistic winning budget based on what you need to win the race, without any fat or luxuries in it. Even though it may be tough to ultimately achieve, it's still the goal that drives your entire fundraising strategy.

You should focus on what you need to win and constantly shoot for that. It's easy to fall back on a barebones budget, but if it's inadequate to win the race, it can mislead you.

Use a barebones budget only when you have reached a brick wall and know you won't have the money to fund your desired budget. When that happens, it's usually a bad sign but is not necessarily fatal. Often, your opponents will have the same problem.

You can also include various options (for example: Option A includes three weeks of TV and two weeks of radio, Option B includes two weeks of TV and three weeks of radio, etc.) in your overall budget scenario.

Initial budgets should be simply structured around line items and a timeline cash flow schedule. Even though we can talk about the details forever, for the purposes of this guide we're suggesting a simple, quick, understandable approach that can be beefed up later with more information.

Budget line items should include every possible expenditure, generally centered on two major areas, the public part of the campaign (communications and research) and the behind-the-scenes part of the campaign (organizational and administrative):

1. Communications and research include:
• Television and radio time buys and production;
• Newspaper space buys and production;
• Direct mail, include printing, lists and labels, postage, mail shop, production and design for each piece, for mass mailings as well as smaller, targeted and in-house mail shop efforts;
• Outdoor billboard space, production and printing;
• Printing, design, typesetting and pre-press for brochures, hand cards, tabloids, ballots, letterhead and envelopes, fliers, invitations, yard signs, posters, bumper stickers, body badges, buttons, volunteer cards;
• Telephone banks (first determine if you are going to hire a professional firm or do it with volunteers, the latter is often just as expensive and almost always less efficient than a professional phone system);
• Media training and expert coaching for speeches, interviews, debates (a must for newcomers and experienced pols, alike);
• Photography including photographer's fee, film and processing, make-up and lighting;
• Polling and research, including your first benchmark poll, follow-up surveys, tracking polls, focus groups and specific issue and opposition research activities.

2. Organizational and administrative include:

• Staff salaries, expenses, insurance, taxes;

• Headquarters rent, office supplies, equipment and furniture, daily postage, computer hardware, software, parking, decorations, petty cash, long distance, faxing, refreshments;

• Consultant fees, retainers, expenses;

• Travel, auto rentals, gasoline, airfare, cabs, buses, subways, hotels, meals, tips paid by the candidate and staff;

• Legal, accounting and fees (such as qualifying and candidate filing fees) and costs involving legal compliance and reporting;

• Volunteer activities such as door-to-door canvassing, poll workers, rallies and coffee parties (yes, make no mistake about it, even volunteer activities cost money);

• Subsidies to political organizations to cover your share of campaigning (in some jurisdictions, there are legal restrictions on these activities, so watch out);

• Gifts and donations, such as buying ads in high school football programs and tickets to charitable affairs;

• Voter registration and special absentee programs (be especially careful none of these activities overlap with the direct mail and phone bank line items);

• Election day get-out-the-vote programs (again, beware of possible overlaps).

3. *Keep your options open.*

You may want to build options into your campaign budget. For example, you may figure you need to produce and air two TV spots, one an introductory "bio" spot which features the candidate's personal background and the other an attack spot against your opponent. However, if your opponent attacks you, you may need an answer spot, which would require adding the cost of producing and airing a third spot. That can be budgeted as an optional line item.

4. *Think mobilization versus persuasion.*

A fundamental budgeting decision has to do with your campaign strategy. Will you emphasize mobilization or persuasion?

Mobilization is about getting your support base to the polls. It most often involves grassroots organization, direct voter contact (mail, phones, canvassing) and election day turnout.

Persuasion is about reaching undecided voters with messages that will swing them your way. It most often involves TV, radio and newspaper advertising, message-oriented direct mail and press/public relations initiatives.

If you're an unknown candidate in a multi-candidate primary, your budget should emphasize persuasion since you do not yet have a large, defined voter base to mobilize. Your most important job is to convince voters who you don't know that you're the best candidate.

If you're a well-known general election candidate in a constituency where your party has a big advantage, your budget should emphasize mobilization since you already have a large support base. Your most important job is to identify, consolidate, organize, energize and then turn out on election day your pre-existing constituency.

Almost every campaign requires both mobilization and persuasion activities. It is a matter of balancing the two needs in a way that works with your overall strategic goals.

5. *Remember: Timing is everything.*

Obviously a key part of strategy and message, timing is an integral part of the overall campaign plan. Timing is often the most difficult aspect of planning message communications and strategic implementation. It is also related to available money, which is why a cash-flow schedule is vital.

The timeline schedule should be broken into smaller and smaller time frames as you get closer to election day and spending activity increases.

See Appendix C with a line-item budget work sheet you can use in your campaign.

★ Chapter 7

Raising the Money
Seven principles of candidate fundraising

Most candidates detest asking for money. In fact, some dislike it so much they don't do it. But if you don't raise money, you're forced to do one of two things: fund your campaign out of your own pocket, or run without money. The former is OK if you're wealthy and can afford to write a big check as Jon Corzine did when he spent $60 million of his own money to win a Senate seat from New Jersey in 2000. The latter is OK if you're a safe incumbent or a prohibitive frontrunner running against an unknown long shot who has no capacity to fund a serious campaign against you. But if you're in any other situation, it's not OK.

Like it or not, candidates in most elections bear the brunt of fundraising. Unless you're running for a highly competitive U.S. Senate seat or in one of 30 or 40 congressional districts that have been targeted by national party committees and interest groups for wide-open combat, it's unlikely that other forces will assume all or most of the burden for you.

Most contributors want to be personally asked by candidates. They want incumbent and future public officials to know who they are and, in some cases, to owe them a debt of thanks.

After you've budgeted your campaign, you have to turn your attention to identifying and reaching potential contributors.

There are four ways for candidates to raise money:

• *Ask* others for contributions by calling them on the phone or meeting with them in person.

• *Ask* others to ask their friends and associates for contributions.

• *Ask* others to organize fundraising events and to sell tickets to their friends and associates.

• *Ask* others for contributions through direct mail, mass telephoning and Internet appeals.

As you can readily see, fundraising is about asking. It's a numbers game. The more people you ask for money, the more money you'll raise.

Of course, there's more to it than that. You must ask the right people the right way. That takes preparation, coordination and organization.

There are many things that can be said about how candidates should solicit money. Here, we'll concentrate on seven fundamental principles. If you master them, you'll raise all the money you'll need. It's that simple. And as you'll see, that hard.

1. Candidate frame of mind.

The candidate's attitude is critical. It is the linchpin of the entire fundraising effort.

If a candidate approaches fundraising with misery and dread, the results will tend to be miserable and dreadful. If a candidate approaches the task with a positive, hopeful, upbeat attitude, the results will reflect it.

Most candidates start off their money chase with knots in their stomachs, shaking their heads in despair, wondering where the first and last dollar will come from.

This is the wrong way to look at it.

The right way was expressed by Republican fundraising consultant Dan Morgan, who made this compelling point at a *Campaigns & Elections* training seminar: "*Everyone in your district wants to give you money.*" That's the best, most constructive perspective you can have. Once you see it that way, then it's just a matter of figuring out who they are, where they are, how to ask them, how to motivate them, how much to ask them for and when to ask them.

Don't assume that *nobody* wants to give you money. Assume that *everybody* wants to give you money. By so doing, you can see the sources open up.

Democratic consultant Cathy Allen summed up the art and science of political fundraising this way: "Raising money requires discipline. It requires organization. It means being persistent. Asking for money and getting it also requires good timing, a sense of humor and enough self-esteem that you can handle rejection as much as 70 percent of the time over the course of a campaign day."

Allen adds, "Everyone should help with fundraising." That means all of your volunteers and political supporters and business associates should be involved in the fundraising process.

Notice that both Morgan and Allen began their advice with the same word: *Everyone.*

When thinking about where you can find the money you need, expand your horizon and broaden your view. Don't limit yourself. Think big – and wide.

2. Scheduling and time management.

Some candidates dial for dollars in snippets of time. They catch five minutes here, 30 minutes there, and use the time to ask for money.

In my own campaigns, and working with many other candidates, I've found that the snippet approach doesn't work.

Candidates need to be given *large blocs of time* that are set aside solely for fundraising, without disturbance or distraction.

Large blocs of time – whether it's a four- or five-hour half day, a 10- or 12-hour full day or a full week of 10- or 12-hour days – gives candidates the span they need to *focus*. And focus is critical.

The late consultant Matt Reese used to advise candidates to divide each day's schedule into three time blocs: morning, afternoon and evening. That adds up to 21 blocs a week and about 80-90 blocs a month. These time blocs should then be targeted to specific activities, reflecting the campaign's pressing needs and priorities, such as raising money.

3. Donor research.

Knowing a lot about potential donors – their interests, occupations, past donation history, personal and professional relationships – is crucial to figuring out how and when to ask them for money, and at what level.

Allen expressed this need very well when she said, "The goal of all good high-donor fundraising is to know *more about the people you call* than they will ever know about you."

That means: Do your homework before you ask. Get your lists together and do the needed research. Go through past contributor records. Find out who gave to whom, and how much. Ask your supporters and volunteers if they know these people.

The key is to find a contributor's hot button. They all have one.

The best story I recall from my own fundraising was the day I walked into a large office building to meet a potential donor, a prominent corporate executive I did not know. As I was standing in the building's lobby looking for his name and suite number on the directory, a local lawyer who was supporting my candidacy just happened to walk by. He asked me what I was doing, and I told him who I was on the way to see. Fortunately for me, he knew the man very well and gave me a nugget of information that proved to be vital. "Education is his issue, make sure you hit it hard," he advised. After thanking him, I got into the elevator and went upstairs.

"Education, education, education," I thought to myself, as I was ushered into the executive's impressive office. After pleasantries were exchanged, he predictably asked me why I wanted to be in the legislature. My answer: "Education. I want to fight to make our schools better."

As soon as I got those simple words out of my mouth, this tall and distinguished man stood up by his desk, raised his eyes to heaven and said with unbridled enthusiasm, "Finally! A politician who understands how important education is!"

After a brief chat, he handed me a $1,000 check and said he'd raise more. Over the next several weeks, he gathered over $10,000 for my campaign.

If I hadn't run into that lawyer in the lobby, I would have gone into the executive's office and talked about 10 different things, with education as only one of them. But knowing what my potential donor's hot button was, I was able to hit it first and hard, to the right effect.

They say the key to real estate is location, location, location. Well, the key to asking for money is information, information, information.

4. The hit.

When you make your pitch for money, use the following three techniques:

(a) Tie the money you're asking for to a *specific need*. Whether it's TV time, a direct mail piece or a big radio splash, it's a good idea to tell your donor what you're trying to fund with his or her money. This gives the pitch form and purpose.

(b) Tie the specific need to a *deadline*. You don't want to seem desperate (desperate people get no respect), but you do want to create a sense of immediacy, even urgency, for the money. Explain that the TV time needs to be bought by tomorrow at noon. Or that the radio splash needs to start in three days. Or the direct mail piece needs to be printed and processed by the end of the week to get it out before election day.

(c) Tie the specific need and deadline to a *requested amount*. "I need to buy $20,000 in TV time tomorrow and I'm trying to get 20 people to each come up with $1,000 for it."

Giving a potential donor a dollar level sets the stakes. When providing a specific dollar amount, make sure you shoot a little high, but not ridiculously high. If you think someone is good for $500 to $1,000, ask for the upper limit. If you're not sure, take a calculated risk on the high side.

You never want to leave anything on the table. There's nothing worse than asking a $1,000 donor for $500.

If you do ask for too little, and your donor gives you a quick OK, without breaking a sweat or blinking an eye, and you instantly feel like you've let him or her off too light, keep going. After the donor agrees to the $500 figure, ask if you can count on him or her again in a few weeks when you'll need another $500 for a mail piece you're planning.

If at first you succeed, try, try again for even more!

As Allen advised, "Your job is not so much to convince a

prospective donor that she or he should support and contribute to your campaign. Your job is to *negotiate* the amount."

Here's something else experienced fundraisers will tell you, echoing advice that commercial sales pros always stress: After you make the specific request for money ("Can I count on you for $1,000?"), shut up. Keep silent, no matter how long it takes. Wait for the donor to speak next. *The first one to make a sound loses.*

The moment after you make the request, you've got maximum leverage. Don't then give the donor something else to talk about. Don't distract from, or confuse, the moment, even if the silence is long and deafening. Stay focused on the request. Keep him or her focused on the request. Silence may really be golden.

Some donors may say no, but very few of them like to say no. Don't let them off the hook. Make them say "no" or "yes." *Force* the choice.

5. Timing.

As we've noted, a fundamental tenet of fundraising is not to leave anything on the table. That means don't let a potential $1,000 or $2,000 contributor off the hook by getting the individual to buy one or two $100 tickets to a fundraiser. This requires that you ask for the $1,000 or $2,000 contribution *before* you or someone else asks the donor to purchase an event ticket or two.

It's a matter of timing. Harvest high-dollar donors first. *Then* go back and try to sell them event tickets. If you do it the other way around, you'll sell the tickets but may miss out on the larger contribution.

This is another reason you need to research your donors, contact them early and set the stakes for a specific request. Maximize each donor's potential – that's what fundraising is all about.

6. The pick-up.

When someone agrees to give you money, get it *immediately*. If that means standing over them while they write the check, do it. If that means sending someone over by foot or by car to pick it up, do it. If that means instantly processing the donation on the Internet using a credit card, do it. Remember, time is money.

By all means, have a pick-up mechanism in place. When the donor says OK, get the money without a minute's delay.

When I was running for office, I called a local home builder one morning and asked him for money. He committed on the phone to giving me a $1,500 contribution. He told me he'd be in his office between five and six o'clock that afternoon, but that if I couldn't make it, he'd be there the next morning with the check.

Well, I was very busy that afternoon and figured I'd go by his office the next morning to pick it up. When I got there the next morning, he wasn't there. Neither was the check. I called him for days and finally got a return call. He expressed his regrets, but said his wife had sued him for divorce the afternoon we first talked, freezing his bank accounts thereby making it impossible for him to now give me the money. I subsequently learned that he was telling the truth.

If I had gone there that afternoon, instead of waiting until the next morning, I would have gotten the check and could have cashed it in time. But because I let it slide, assuming wrongly that it could wait until the next morning, I lost the money.

In political fundraising, there is no tomorrow.

Years later, I heard another, even more telling – and sad – story. A gubernatorial candidate back in the 1960s was trying to get a $50,000 contribution from a wealthy retired businessman in his state. In those days, when you could run a good race for governor in a small state on a $250,000 or $300,000 budget, fifty grand was a lot of money.

After the candidate spent hours with the elderly gentleman answering every question under the sun, he finally got the commitment he wanted. In fact, the donor was prepared to write out the check as they were starting dinner. The candidate, gentleman that he was, said he didn't want to interrupt dinner and could wait to do the paperwork until after they were finished eating. Well, minutes later, the old man collapsed and died. And with that, so did the $50,000 contribution.

7. *Organization and follow-up.*

In addition to knowing how and when to ask for money, you also need an organization in place to:

(a) Build donor prospecting lists. You can't call someone unless you have a list with full contact information. Systematize this process. Set up a good database management system of both past and potential donors that includes every bit of recordable information you have on each person.

(b) Send advance information packets to prospective donors. These packets should be sent to donors *before* you call them. They provide an introduction and should generally include the candidate's biography, positions on relevant issues and something about how the candidate plans to win. You want the prospect to feel like he or she is "on the inside" and "in the know."

In most campaigns, it's essential that you look like a winner, or at least seem to have a serious shot at winning. Contributors need to be motivated before they will give. Anything you can do to motivate them is important. Providing the right advance information can be a key to getting them charged up.

Contributors are motivated by a lot of things, including: ideology, friendship, personal access, party success, hatred of the opposition, peer pressure and candidate electability. Donors want to feel like they're making a difference. They also prefer to be "on the winning side."

(c) Send personalized thank-you letters every time someone pledges help or sends money. Mail these letters the *same day* you get the pledge or the check.

(d) Handle all public reporting and legal compliance. This usually requires keeping thorough, accurate records of each contributor and various information about them (name, address, business affiliation, phone number, etc.).

(e) Go back and ask past contributors for more money. Remember: Your best fundraising list is always your past donor list.

For donors who have legally "maxed out" on how much they can give in elections where there are legal contribution caps, call and ask them to help you find *new* sources.

★ Chapter 8

The Guarantee System

A sure-fire technique for any candidate to raise big bucks – fast

At the start of most political campaigns, there is a need for a quick infusion of cash. That's a daunting prospect for candidates and their staffs. For some, it's a seemingly impossible dream.

But there is a way to meet this brutal demand – without selling your soul or breaking any laws. I call it the "guarantee system." If done in the right way at the right time for the right reasons, it can work like a charm.

The "guarantee system" is a way to get prospective contributors to write the biggest possible checks at the earliest possible moment. The key to the system is giving select, early contributors a chance to get their money back. It's a way to soften the hit, which allows you to ratchet up the size of the request.

This system makes it easier for the candidate to "guarantee" from the outset that the campaign will have adequate initial funding. Once that's done, the campaign and the candidate can concentrate on raising a volume of smaller donations over time.

Make It Easy on Yourself

When asking for the money under the "guarantee system," explain that it's a loan to the campaign – 100 percent of which will be repaid if you win and *only* if you win. Make that clear and spell it out in a simple agreement. In addition to this repay-if-you-win pledge, you should also give your benefactor a supply of tickets to a pre-election fundraising event that he or she can sell to others as a way to get their money back *before* the election, regardless of the outcome.

So, when benefactors write checks, they do so knowing that they have a shot at getting all or some of their money back. This reduces the "sticker shock" for potential contributors, thus making it easier for them to rationalize large contributions.

Notice, here, that you're not asking for mere pledges or promissory notes; you're asking for cash-on-the-barrel.

The repayment aspect is rooted in the premise that fundraising after a win is much easier than fundraising at the start of a campaign when the outcome may be very much in doubt; therefore, the commitment that you will repay the loan after you win is a credible one.

Of course, as an ethical matter, you should never seek or accept a check so large that you do not believe it could be refunded after winning.

Group Effort

It's vital that you only use the "guarantee system" for a select number of contributors as part of an early group effort to "guarantee" initial funding of your campaign.

If you overuse this approach, you may find yourself in a position where all your "contributors" expect to be treated as "lenders" and will want their money back after you win, which may not be affordable. Keep in mind that many of your rich, rabid contributors will write maximum checks without incentives, so don't use the "guarantee" sweetener unless it's necessary.

If you're going to use this system, use it early before other fundraising takes place. You want to employ it to leverage up what donors would ordinarily give. If you wait too long to use this approach, you risk giving a potential $2,000 donor a chance to get off the hook with a $200 check.

When scheduling the fundraising event for "guarantee" benefactors to give them an additional chance to get back their money, make sure it's very late in the campaign. You don't want them to sell tickets to people who would give you money anyway; you want your benefactors to reach new people *they* know that you may not know, thereby expanding the size of your fundraising network and not just substituting one contribution for another.

Some may ask whether the campaign should consider prearranging a loan process with a local bank for contributors under this system as another way to make it easier on the donor. On this, extreme caution is advised. In the post-Bert Lance era, new federal banking rules have clamped down on the ability of financial institutions to make loans that will be used to fund political campaigns.

Before you do anything in this regard, you must explore your ideas with knowledgeable lawyers, bankers and election authorities to make sure your plans do not run afoul of some highly complicated and restrictive regulations.

The safe approach is to stay away from arranging loans for other people, not only from a legal standpoint but also from the standpoint that introduction of the element of "loans" (that must be repaid to the bank regardless of the election outcome) may result in contributors wanting the candidate to co-sign debt instruments. This, of course, opens up issues involving the candidate being responsible for repaying the money – win or lose – which violates the repay-only-if-you-win concept.

Don't complicate the process and don't push the edges of the law. The idea of the "guarantee system" is simply to make it easier to raise large donations early, not to play games with too-clever-by-half schemes that could land you in the penitentiary.

How Much Do You Need?

To use the "guarantee system," the first thing you must decide is how much money you need to get your campaign off the ground. Let's say you're running for the state legislature with a $150,000 budget. You may want to pull in one-third of your budget through the "guarantee system," building a $50,000 initial war chest. If you're running for Congress, and the overall fundraising goal for your primary campaign is $500,000, your initial war chest goal may be, say, $200,000.

The maximum allowable individual contribution under the law governing your election is crucial. If you're running for a *federal* office (U.S. House, Senate, president), it's set by federal law and administered by the Federal Election Commission. If you're running for a *nonfederal* office – governor or state legislator or school board – it depends on your state's law and any applicable local rules. Some elections have no limits at all.

Most campaign finance laws treat loans the same as they do contributions for purposes of caps. The "guarantee system's" only-if-you-win loan concept is not a way to skirt campaign laws, but merely a way to make it less painful for large donors to spring big – and early.

Once you've taken these first steps, you can determine how much total money you need from a "guarantee system" to build your initial war chest.

In the state legislative race example, let's assume that there are no donation caps in your state. You may determine that to raise the initial $50,000, your aim is to get 10 people to each put up $5,000.

In a large statewide race for governor without caps, for instance, the "guarantee system" strategy may entail getting 40 $50,000 benefactors to produce a $2 million initial war chest.

In a campaign where there are legal donation limits (let's say $2,000 per person), your goal may be to get $2,000 from each of 50 individuals and $4,000 from each of 50 couples to fund an initial $300,000 war chest.

In races where contribution caps are low (say, under $1,000), the "guarantee system" has diminished effect because there is less opportunity to build a substantial war chest from a small number of donors. In states with high caps ($5,000 or more) or those with no caps, the "guarantee system" has its greatest potential.

At this point, you may be wondering whether I've ever used this system to actually raise money. The answer is yes, many times. I've used it for my own campaigns and I've helped other candidates use it in their races. In one mayoral race budgeted at $800,000, I used it to bring in nearly $400,000 in two weeks from a dozen "guarantors."

All journeys start with a single step. When it comes to

political fundraising, the "guarantee system" is a good, clean way to break out of the starting gate.

★ Chapter 9

Candidate Door-to-Door Canvassing

In local and district races, this may be your key to victory – if it's done right

I was a 24-year-old candidate for the state House running against an incumbent with loads of organized political support. Fresh out of law school, I had no political connections, no name recognition and, according to the local wags, no chance.

One thing I did have was time. There were seven months between my getting into the race and election day. That, I decided, was a precious resource that could make the difference.

My strategy was simple: Go to the people that the incumbent had ignored. While he was hobnobbing with politicians and lobbyists in the state capital, I'd go into the neighborhoods of our district and meet the voters face to face.

My goal was to knock on every door that had at least one live voter behind it, all 12,000 of them.

So I mapped out a plan with these goals in mind: First, I'd cover 100 percent of the district. The area was a heterogeneous mixture of urbanites, suburbanites and even a small fishing village, covering a wide range of lower- to upper-middle income voters, two-thirds white and one-third black. The door-to-door districtwide canvass was central to my campaign message of staying in touch with average people. I couldn't skimp. Not only did I need to reach every household just to get my name recognition up, I needed to do it so that I could say I did it.

Second, I'd implement a system of instant, personalized

follow-up. To enhance the impact of the canvass, I'd mail out a personal note every evening to every voter in every household I had visited that day. This would seal the contacts I had made and extend the reach of the canvass to people who weren't home.

Third, inoculate myself from the biggest weakness I had as a candidate: extreme youth. Consequently, it was better for me to canvass alone, without anyone else tagging along. I didn't want to look like a kid in tow of an adult, or even worse, a kid surrounded by a bunch of other kids. Because my campaign theme stressed personal independence, going it alone was strategic reinforcement. To help offset my youthful appearance, my campaign literature delivered a serious, substantive message and provided detailed biographical information.

To project maturity, I wore a navy blue suit, white dress shirt and a businesslike red tie – even in the oppressive New Orleans heat of July and August.

I was sweating so badly one steamy day that I had to apologize for the perspiration dropping off my face onto the brochures I was handing out. I knew everything was OK, though, when a grisly middle-aged man in an undershirt reassured me not to worry. "I sweat for a living every day, too," he said.

Singing in the Rain
The hardest doorbell for a candidate to ring is the first one. Canvassing takes an enormous amount of time and a serious commitment. It's easy to find an excuse as to why you can't do it. In fact, I didn't start my canvassing until two weeks after I had scheduled – I was highly successful in finding good reasons to delay the start of the long march.

Because I planned to reach every household anyway, and wanted to give an impression of being everywhere, I decided to work the district randomly – without targeting my visits based on geographical coverage. My plan was to go into every part of the district every few days. I also didn't want to follow a discernible pattern that could have alerted the opposition to where I was working. I couldn't afford to give them a chance to strike before or after my sorties.

Fortunately, my district had plenty streets that were four to five blocks long with about 40 houses on each side. I would start on the odd-numbered side and go up the street then return down the even-numbered side. In fact, we arranged my walk lists so that the odd and even numbered houses were on separate sheets.

It would take about two hours to do one of these streets, which meant that I could do one between six and eight o'clock in the evening (that was an easy one-street night) or one at five o'clock and a second one at seven o'clock (that was a more strenuous two-street night). During daylight savings time, two-street nights were much easier because only the last 30 to 60 minutes of each evening's canvass would be in the dark. One-street nights allowed me to make an evening speaking engagement or dinner.

On Saturdays, I'd usually start at eleven o'clock in the morning, break at one, then resume at about three in the afternoon. On Sundays, I'd often canvass between three and five o'clock in the afternoon, break and return at six. When it got closer to the election, I'd often add another hour or two to the Saturday and Sunday schedules and continue until 9:30 on week nights. On a few nights, when I was running behind schedule, I found myself still knocking at near ten o'clock, which was too late.

Some political operatives will tell you never to knock on doors between five and seven o'clock because it's dinner hour. That's a fine rule if you don't intend to reach any more than a minimal number of households. But if you have a big district, you'll find that the only way you can meet enough people at home is to work through the early evenings.

Candidates, by the way, can get away with some things volunteers can't. A campaign worker who interrupts someone's dinner may receive a chilly reception; when it's the candidate, the reception is usually much better.

Of course, it depends on the neighborhood. In middle-class neighborhoods where both husband and wife work during the day, it's usually a waste of time to hit these areas before five o'clock. In upper income communities, you'll find that daytime canvassing brings you in touch with a lot of maids and housekeepers but few voters who actually reside at that address.

One of the best times to canvass as a candidate is on rainy days. Voters feel sorry for you when you're dripping wet on their doormat under an umbrella; they appreciate the effort. (Fortunately, most people don't stop and think about what a crazed, ambitious nut would do such a thing.) So, when there was a chance of a shower, I'd jump with joy! It was serious vote-getting climate and I wouldn't miss a minute of it.

Sorry I Missed You

When I met a voter at his or her front door, my pitch was short and simple. I'd introduce myself with a handshake, explain I was running for state representative, and ask for their "help" – figuring that help was harder to refuse and sounded less political than "vote" or "support." I'd then hand them a four-paneled black-and-white brochure. If they had nothing substantive to say, I'd thank them and leave. That's it. I didn't attempt to engage people in long conversations about issues. I wanted this to be a personal meeting of like-minded citizens, not a sales pitch from a politician. When voters wanted substantive information, I'd happily give it to them, answering their questions and spelling out my views on issues.

When there was no one home, I'd leave a brochure with a note that said, "*I was in your neighborhood today as part of my door-to-door campaign for State Representative. Sorry I missed you. Ron.*" The notes were paper clipped to the folder and I'd leave them in a conspicuous place near each household's front door with the handwritten message showing.

Most people forget that in a door-to-door canvass, at best you only meet about 30 percent of the voters in that area. That's because about 40 percent of houses will have no one home, or at least no one who answers the door. In the 60 percent of the households you do make contact with, they will often average at least two voters each. If only one voter comes to the door, you're only personally meeting half of the voters in those houses. Those numbers are only a rough rule of thumb because they will vary greatly by neighborhood demographics and cultural differences between constituencies.

"Sorry I missed you" notes are, therefore, very important. As are the follow-up letters you will send to voters who weren't home or whom you didn't have a chance to meet.

Doing It in the Dark

Along the way, I had things happen to me that only happen to a candidate for public office. Like the time a woman opened her door and a gigantic, ferocious, growling, foaming-from-the-mouth dog – at the time it looked like a charging rhinoceros – was straining to get at me; the woman did her best to hold the hound back by grabbing his tail until finally she was forced to close the door and speak to me through the mail slot.

Then there was the time when a child of about 7 or 8 answered the door. I told him I wanted to see his parents. He led me into their darkened home, through the entry foyer and back into their family room. It was pitch-black without any lights. The boy then introduced me to his parents, who I couldn't see and who couldn't see me. I could hear them rustling around as they expressed shock that their son would invite a stranger into their home. Finally, somebody had the presence of mind to turn on a lamp instead of getting a pistol, and all went well from then on.

On occasion, dogs could be a little annoying; especially when they chase you from house-to-house, barking loudly at you along the route. I never did it, but some candidates I know would bring along dog biscuits they'd use as "hush money." It makes you understand the travails of a letter carrier.

Not only do you run into odd situations when going door to door, but you also have a chance to meet a lot of nice people, some of whom will become your firmest supporters and best friends. Going into the homes and neighborhoods of a constituency is a way for a candidate to build a personal grassroots organization from the ground up. There is no substitute for the powerful impact of this kind of effort.

Magic of Follow-Up

The key to an effective candidate canvass is an efficient, personalized follow-up system of mailings.

To capture the necessary information I'd need to sign up volunteers and to target follow-up letters, I had my walk lists organized by age with party affiliations for each household's voter.

For example, if the Miller family had four voters with one of them a 50-year-old man, one of them a 48-year-old woman, one of them a 22-year-old woman and one of them a 78-year-old man, I'd assume – usually accurately – that this house was occupied by a husband, wife, daughter and father-in-law. That was vital information, because it allowed me to figure out which registered voter was Chuck (the 50-year-old Democrat), which one was Fred (the 78-year-old Republican), which one was Ruth (the 48-year-old Republican) and which one was Mary (the 22-year-old Independent). This kind of information makes it possible to gear the follow-up letters directly to the person you actually met.

To do this easily, my walk list had to be arranged accordingly:

STREET	ADDRESS	VOTER NAME	AGE	PARTY	MY CODE
Hardy St.	2204	John Smith	38	R	A
		Mary Smith	36	R	D
	2206	Jane Baker	73	D	C
	2208	Bill Brown	53	R	B
		Cecila Brown	50	R	D
		Patsy Brown	22	D	D

Voter name, address, age and party affiliation was information readily available on lists candidates could purchase from the local registrar of voters.

To make it easier and quicker for me to comprehend, birth years (1955, 1963, 1974, etc.) were converted to current ages so I didn't have to waste time calculting them in my head as I walked up to each house.

Easy as A, B, C, D and E

After leaving each house, I'd immediately fill in a code des-
ignation (A through E) for each voter in the household while
walking toward the next stop.

• If someone committed support and volunteered to put
up a sign, work in headquarters, donate money or send out
postcards, I'd code that person as an A. (It should be noted
that about two-thirds of the volunteers and sign locations we
recruited in the entire campaign came from my canvass.)

• If someone specifically and clearly committed to vote
for me, but didn't offer to volunteer beyond the vote, I'd code
that person a B.

• If someone did not specifically say they would vote for
me, even if they were very nice and *seemed* to be favorable, I
coded them as a C – which meant they were uncommitted or
undecided. Most voters received C's, except in the last few
weeks before the election when the number of B's increased.

• If there was no one home, I'd code every voter in the
household as a D. If I met only one voter in a multiple-voter
household, I'd code any voter I did *not* meet as a D.

• Voters who said they supported the opposition were
coded with an E.

These codes were the basis of the follow-up letter system,
which was critical to the whole strategy. Each one would say
something like:

"A" letter – "Your offer of help for my campaign for State
Representative is greatly appreciated. We'll be in touch soon
to get you involved. Your kindness and generosity will always
be remembered – and will make a vital difference. Together,
we'll win this race!"

"B" letter – "Your commitment of support for my candidacy for State Representative is greatly appreciated. Working
together, we can improve state government for the people of
our area. Your vote will make the crucial difference on election day. Your kindness and your willingness to put your trust
and confidence in me will always be remembered. "

"C" letter – "This is just a note to thank you for receiving

me at your home yesterday. I greatly appreciate your time and interest and hope, in the days ahead, I'll be able to earn your trust, your friendship and your vote. Again, thanks very much. I hope to see you again soon."

"D" letter – "I'm sorry I missed you at home yesterday when I visited your neighborhood as part of my door-to door campaign for State Representative. I'm enclosing some material about my personal qualifications and positions on issues I thought you may find useful. Again, thanks very much for your interest. I look forward to meeting you and, hopefully, to earning your vote in the days ahead."

"E" letter – "Thank you for your candid explanation of your position in this race for State Representative. While I wish I could count you as a supporter, I'm nevertheless appreciative that you have taken a stand and take an active interest. Perhaps along the way we can join together and work as partners to make our city and state a better place. Again, thanks."

Each letter was short, personal and contained minimal political rhetoric.

If a voter raised a specific issue during the visit, asked a question or made a memorable comment, then I'd often pen a handwritten note on the follow-up typed letter. For example, if a voter talked about his or her support for tougher penalties for violent criminals, I would write a note that reiterated my agreement with that concern.

While it would be nice to be able to write personal notes on *every* letter, time won't permit it if your district is too large. To avoid getting bogged down in endless details when running in a large area, typed notes on monarch-sized letterhead with actual signatures suffice.

To make sure the recipient of the letter knew that I had personally signed it, I'd always sign the letters on a surface a little soft to make sure that the writing would press through the paper so that if you ran your fingers on the back of the page you'd feel it.

Each night, I'd bring the walk lists with my follow-up letter codes and an occasional comment by each name to my campaign office. Usually, a volunteer would type the letters that same evening. In some cases, they'd type the letters the next morning. In every case, we'd mail out all the follow-up letters within 24 hours of the previous day's canvass. We only missed that goal a few times.

The canvass also served as a useful theme for the campaign's media advertising. Our first TV spot featured photos of me talking to voters at their front doors.

The spot's copy opened with the authoritative and eloquent tones of the late Barton Heymann, a legendary voice-over professional, who explained, "Since June, Ron Faucheux has been walking through New Orleans East, campaigning for State Representative the hard way. Person to person. Door to door." It provided a backdrop to the campaign's central message of an out-of-touch incumbent being opposed by an in-touch challenger.

The TV spot, by the way, ran off and on during the three weeks before the primary election. After it had aired a few days, public reaction to my canvassing changed markedly. As I walked the streets, people would now stop, point and say, "Hey, you're the guy on TV!" It made all the difference.

The advertising flight brought all those months of lonely shoe-leather combat into the bright focus of the picture tube. And it seemed to be coming together.

Making the Difference

Every story has a moral. So here it is for this one: *Candidate canvassing works.* But it works best when you take care of the details, keep in mind your overall strategic needs and organize a precise and swift follow-up system designed to seal commitments of support, reinforce personal contacts and distribute campaign materials.

Of course, I wouldn't have told this story if I had lost the race. (Political war stories are usually confined to those with happy endings.) For the record, I ran first in a six-candidate field in the open primary, topping the incumbent 42 percent to 39 percent. That shocked the local political community. It also shocked my opponent, who had done little door-to-door himself before the primary but stepped up his canvassing effort in the runoff (general election) – when it was a little too late.

I won the general election with 55 percent of the vote.

If I hadn't knocked on those doors, or if I had knocked on substantially fewer of those doors, or if I hadn't used an efficient mail follow-up system, I wouldn't have made it.

Nothing beats candidate door-to-door. *Nothing.*

★ Chapter 10

Hiring Consultants

What to look for when picking your professional campaign team

The best place to get insights on how to hire consultants is from the consultants themselves. They understand the strengths and weaknesses of practitioners in their business better than anybody.

When I've asked consultants how they'd advise smart candidates to make successful hires, they've offered a broad perspective, assuredly colored by their own experiences, egos, victories and defeats. But one factor stood out. "Chemistry is critical," said Arthur J. Hackney, a media consultant based in Washington, D.C. "If you and a consultant don't spark personally, it won't be a good fit .... A candidate needs a consultant who can lay it on the line, read your heart and translate your fire into media that burns just as brightly. Your consultant must be the one voice you hear forsaking all others, until-death-do-you-part."

"Candidates should feel comfortable with the consultant they hire," said Tony Payton, a consultant based in Arlington, Virginia. "They ought to feel like they're on the same wavelength." To explain his point, Payton recalled the story of an Arkansas candidate who "once told me it was important for the candidate and consultant to match noses. I never knew what he meant, but I think it was that things should smell the same to both of them."

Florida-based pollster Dave Beattie has in focus groups asked numerous candidates about picking consultants. He's found that "most candidates rehired a consultant because they liked their personality. Consultants can maximize their chance of being hired – getting referrals and retaining the candidate's trust – by realizing that personality does matter and there are some candidates that would be better served by someone with a different personality."

Pollster Brad Bannon has stressed the need to build teams that get along and work well together. "The longer that I am in this business, the more I am convinced that campaigns that build strong teams win elections. In other words, hire consultants that you are personally comfortable with and work well with the other consultants as part of a team." Bannon warns against "shotgun marriages that outside forces try to arrange for you." He says, "Building a campaign team also means keeping away from consultants who think they know all the answers. The right answers to winning an election are a product of strategy sessions with contributions from the many campaign specialists that make up a successful modern campaign."

Just as personal chemistry is crucial, professional confidence is also key. Said pollster Mark Mellman about hiring media consultants: "The most important question a candidate should ask is, 'Do I trust them to tell my story?' More people will come to know more about you through your campaign commercials than in any other way .... You need to have complete confidence that your media consultant will portray you in a way with which you will be happy."

Echoing Mellman's argument, consultants Rick Ridder and Luther Symons have explained, "It is very important that the overall style of the media consultant match that of the candidate and the campaign." As an example, they pointed out, "It will do a candidate little good to hire a media consultant who specializes in humorous ads if the candidate is unable to carry out a humorous script. Similarly, if a realistic assessment of the campaign demonstrates that there will likely be a need to utilize tough, hard-hitting spots, the campaign will be ill-served by hiring a media consultant without experience in producing effective 'negative' ads."

"Candidates must listen beyond the pitch and slick marketing and determine who they trust to best present them and their ideas to the public," counsels consultant Nelson Dollar. "Take your time and interview as many consultants as possible, as early as possible, even if you're just testing the waters."

Another criterion to consider is the ability of a consultant to be strictly objective, unaffected by the emotions of the moment. This is especially important when it comes to hiring pollsters and analysts. They will be called upon, over and over, to look beyond personal friendships and partisan affiliations for the hard reality presented in their data. That's not always easy to do when the candidate has a need for affirmation or, even worse, hero-worship.

"Politicians generally want people to like them," observed Ridder and Symons. "This can be a serious detriment when choosing a pollster. This is one instance in life when you want someone who is willing to tell you the truth ... as opposed to sugar-coating facts and telling you what they believe you want to hear." They added that "a good pollster needs to be the most dispassionate member of the team."

The hiring process can take time, and is often frustrating for candidates who don't know what to look for in the stream of ad firms, pollsters, general consultants, direct mail producers, fundraisers and telephone vendors who come calling, seeking business. Nonetheless, it is crucial to winning the election. "Your campaign is a matter of political life or death: Hire someone like you would a brain surgeon, not based just on price," ominously advises media consultant Karl Struble.

Big Decision

In addition to chemistry, confidence and objectivity, creativity and competence are also considerations, especially when reviewing possible media consultants, who will in effect serve as the campaign's advertising agency and communications ramrod.

Selecting a media consultant is "a big decision. Treat it that way," recommends consultant Jim Duffy. It can also be a time-consuming decision. Most media firms send potential clients reels of ads they've produced as a way to promote their abilities. "Don't just look at the promotional reels," cautions Duffy. "Talk to the firm's winners and losers, find out how much time they spent on each race. Don't just talk to the candidates, talk to the campaign managers as well. You want to know how involved they were in the races."

"Most campaigns are bad consumers," surmises Struble. "They often use a consultant's demo reel as a barometer of a firm's creativity or work product. It's not. Any decent consultant can piece together a string of high concept ads that sizzle or evoke emotion, but that's not what most of your ads will be like."

Struble goes on to suggest that "a better yardstick is to request all the ads produced for a winning and losing campaign, including ads that have not aired. Ask for the ads with slates to determine if there is a break in numbers on the slates. This may indicate a firm is hiding weak ads or had to make numerous changes to please a campaign. The average quality of a whole campaign reel is a much better indicator of what your ads will resemble, not the studs on the demo reel."

Dollar agrees, and adds, "Ideally, a media consultant can provide all the commercials aired by *both* sides through a complete campaign cycle. Campaigns take unexpected turns; you need a consultant that has a proven ability to effectively counter an unexpected attack by an opponent."

"Pay special attention not just to the quality of the ads," emphasizes Struble, but also "look to see if there is a consistent strategic thread to the reel and if the quality diminishes as the campaign progresses." Media strategist Ray Strother, a former president of the American Association of Political Consultants, reinforces the notion that candidates should not evaluate spots in a vacuum, but should look at the larger political context in which they were produced. "Don't fall in love with one cute commercial. Ask questions," he advises.

In judging a consultant's past work, a candidate should remember, says Dan Payne, a Boston-based media consultant, that "it's the work you're paying for, not the presentation, size of the firm or size of the name."

Payne advises candidates to ask themselves, "What role do you, the candidate, want to play in creating and delivering messages? How flamboyant or conservative is your style; how daring or safe do you need to be to win?"

To make these determinations, some candidates ask media consultants to develop a mock campaign for them.

"Show me what you'd do for me," they'll request. But experienced consultants with strong track records often resist doing this. For one thing, they don't want to give campaigns that ultimately don't hire them free ideas. They also don't have the time, or the available information, to develop a campaign as a promotional venture. "Avoid speculative bake-offs, asking a consultant to prepare a sample of what he or she would do for you," says Payne. "This isn't crystal ball gazing."

Instead, Payne advises, look at the tape, observe how the consultant works and find out if you have similar values.

No Time for Training

"Inexperienced candidates and staffs often look for compatibility first, price second and experience last. This is backwards," says Strother. "Hire a hard-nosed professional firm, but first ask about the person who will be assigned to the campaign. Don't pay for training a consultant."

Consultant David Browne suggests inquiring how many people are in the firm you're interviewing and how long they have been there. "As few as 10 years ago, media consultants contented themselves with eight to 12 campaigns in an election cycle. The reputation of the firm was based on the success of a well-known, big-name principal," says Browne. But that has changed. "The trend among media firms, however, has been to work on 20 or more campaigns."

Firms' large client lists require candidates to find out if consultants can handle that much work. "Certainly, if they hire junior level consultants and support people," says Browne. But, he cautions, "This means that after the contract is signed, the campaign is assigned to a member of the team who will do most of the work, calling in the principal or principals only for important meetings and film shoots." Is that what you really want? "Each candidate must decide whether they want deep involvement by their media consultant, and then they must evaluate how much they can expect from each firm they interview," he says.

To make this evaluation, Browne says you should ask media consultants: How many campaigns will the firm contract? How many non-political clients do the consultants represent? How many foreign clients will require their time outside the country? Who will actually write, direct and produce your campaign ads? Will a principal be at every meeting? How often does the firm speak with each client?

Direct participation by the firm's principals is a matter that requires advanced discussion. Duffy suggests asking media consultants if they just showed up to shoot television commercials or were they part of the campaign team? "Find out about each firm's business practices. Do they personally place media or sub the media buying to another firm? Do they mark up spot production or simply bill production at cost? What about commissions and fees, how much and when are they due?"

On the subject of cost, Payne declares: "Don't shop for a Lexus if you can only afford a Toyota. Size matters – but remember principals in big firms can only do so many races; know by name who is going to work on your campaign. Know how many campaigns the firm is doing."

Depending upon your financial and political situation, it may not always be wise to go to Washington, D.C., in search of a "big name" national consultant. When interviewing consultants, suggests direct mail producer Adam Geller, "bring in a mix of Beltway and outside-the-Beltway types. You will learn that some of the brightest, most talented consultants live far away from D.C."

Are big names always the best hires? "With their own success depending so heavily on hype, it's not surprising that candidates often go with the consultant they see on TV, not stopping to think about who's going to be the star of their show," says media consultant John Franzen. "Better to seek out someone who stays studiously behind the scenes, putting the focus on you and refusing to feed the journalists' obsession with campaign process. Also, when crunch time comes, it doesn't help to have the superstar consultant if you can't get him or her on the phone." To avoid bringing on "the overrated and the overextended," suggests Franzen, "there's really no substitute for talking to as many of the consultant's former clients as possible, the winners and the losers."

Media consultant James Farwell, a former business partner of mine, always stressed the importance of "hiring people who have strong analytic and strategic skills." He added, "Too many candidates look for 'feel good' spots on reels with pretty pictures that are devoid of a message that moves voters." Farwell said, "But the positioning of a candidate around the right issues is more important than slick imagery."

Cost is always a factor when financial resources are tough to come by, as they are in most campaigns. Consultant Dollar believes you should try to find out how each consultant deals with money and budgets. "Will the consultant maximize each campaign dollar or will they monopolize the campaign's budget with large fees, commissions and hidden costs?" He continues, "It never ceases to amaze me that the most conservative candidates will hire consultants who run the most wasteful campaigns."

When hiring media firms, always keep in mind that their role in a campaign consists of three distinct components: devising messages and communication strategies; creating and producing ads; and buying the time for those ads and handling the paperwork of media placement.

"Find out if the media placement is done in-house or contracted out," says media consultant Gary Nordlinger. "One is not necessarily better than another, but find out about the buyer and his or her experience. Chances are this person will be handling your largest single expenditure."

Another issue, says Nordlinger, is how fast can the firm turn around spots? In an increasingly competitive world of political media politics, with attacks and counterattacks hurling back and forth, this can be a serious matter. A firm that isn't overextended with too much work, or perhaps one with in-house facilities to do quick post-production chores, may be in a better position to give your campaign the rapid response capability it will need.

Production costs, in addition to the time buys, can be a major budget item. "Be sure to get a handle on production costs. A TV spot can cost from $1,000 to $100,000," says Nordlinger.

Pull the Pieces Together

The ability of a single media firm, or a combination of consultants, to integrate various components of a campaign is important. Fred Wszolek, a political consultant with offices in Virginia, Michigan and South Carolina, cautions, "Don't hire a 'media' consultant. Hire a 'communications' consultant." He explains, "When people think of media consultants, they think only TV. Hire a consultant who understands communications in all its forms. Yes, TV. But radio, mail, phones, the Internet, grassroots and earned media too."

"When hiring a consultant, big name or small fry," says Wszolek, "hire someone who puts all the pieces together into a custom, integrated package, who thinks beyond the boob tube, who knows there's more than one way to skin a political cat."

Another issue in choosing consultants is the influence exerted, often unsolicited and even unwelcome, by fundraisers, party leaders and other consultants. "Understand that informal alliances exist among consultants – certain consultants recommend certain other consultants, for various reasons, not all of which are to your advantage," says Payne.

"Often, winning the fight for employment is testimony more to a firm's sales abilities and insider machinations than political experience and abilities," offers Strother, who did the media for Gary Hart's insurgent 1984 presidential campaign. "It's politics within politics. Cozy deals are often made, and friendships rewarded. Exaggerations and excuses reign supreme."

While "it is important to solicit the thoughts and recommendations of people with experience using consultants," says California-based public relations consultant Joe Cerrell, understand that " ... these people have their own biases ... and their needs may not be the same as yours." Listen to recommendations from others, he says, and "use their advice in conjunction with your research to help you decide on your consultant."

When all is said and done, after you've checked a consultant's references, asked pertinent questions and reviewed their past client lists and work product, it often comes down to your own gut instinct. Is this the person, or firm, I want to go into battle with?

Nordlinger suggests asking yourself, "When it's late October and both you and the consultant are exhausted, who do you want to hear the bad news from?"

The answer to that question will tell you plenty.

Hire an Out-of-Town Consultant?

One of the most perplexing decisions candidates for statewide and local offices face is whether they should hire campaign consultants from out of state.

Out-of-state consultants often offer one big advantage: They have a broad, national perspective on what works and what doesn't in campaigning. They tend to understand the cutting edge of technique and have access to the best available technical talent. They also bring disadvantages: First, distance – they may not be there, in person, when you want them; second, busy schedules – if they're really hot, they may take on too many clients to give all of them adequate attention; third, local knowledge – they may not understand the nuances and customs of the political culture and, worse, may not want to spend the time or effort to learn them.

Local consultants, too, bring both benefits and baggage. Their benefits: First, proximity – they're usually only a short drive away; second, cost – in most cases, they're less expensive than top national practitioners; and third, local knowledge – they grasp the personalities, subtleties and traditions from day one.

Their baggage: They often lack national perspective and an appreciation of advanced techniques; their access to technical talent and technologies may be limited; they may be too immersed in the local scene and, as such, may have too many personal conflicts and lack objectivity.

There is no easy answer to the question as to whether you should stay home or go out of town to hire campaign consultants. But these factors should be considered by candidates and campaign managers as they ponder their options.

The distance problem that comes with an outside pro is

not necessarily that big of a deal in today's society. That's why so many campaigns, large and small, pick the best talent they can find, whether it's nearby or far away.

E-mail, fax machines, cellular phones and video teleconferencing have also made the consulting globe much smaller and have gone a long way to bridging the location/time gap.

The key is to make sure that your out-of-state consultant bears the burden of staying in touch. That means he or she must regularly schedule call-ins and personal meetings. It also means he or she must make an extra effort to be accessible in emergencies and to give you an honest assessment, far in advance, of how much time he or she really will spend on-site in your state or locality.

Busy schedules can cause big problems, and both consultants and clients must beware of them – before they create havoc. In the early stages of election cycles, many consultants fear they won't get enough business, so they sign on a lot of laborious campaigns too early. Many times clients – particularly incumbents – who looked like blow-away winners a year before election day will encounter unexpected troubles along the way and become a major drain on a consultant's mental and physical resources.

In some cases, overextended national consultants delegate important work to second and third tier assistants. When they do, it rightfully upsets clients who were led to believe that the brainpower of the firm's top gun, and not a less-experienced junior associate, would be assigned to the campaign. They only way to ensure against this uncomfortable situation is to raise it clearly and forcefully upfront – and put it into the contract. As soon as you sense that this contract requirement is being bent or broken, put your foot down and be prepared to fire the firm if the breach is bad enough.

Sometimes the member of the firm who is assigned to your account is a matter of compensation. A high-profile $10 million U.S. Senate campaign may believe it has a greater claim on a consultant's time than an obscure $400,000 race for state treasurer. If so, performance expectations need to be clarified at the time the consultant is signed.

Occasionally, a firm's principal will make clear to the

client that his or her time will be limited to only major strategic matters and decisions, and that a proficient junior associate will handle day-to-day chores. If that's the case, it should be specified from the start and reflected in the compensation.

In terms of understanding local political terrain, this depends upon the willingness of the out-of-state consultant to devote the necessary time.

Will an outside consultant know as much about a local political situation as a local one? No, not likely. But that's not the right question.

The right question is: Can an outsider learn enough about local politics to competently handle a campaign? The answer is yes. It's done all the time.

But for this to work, the consultant must: (a) have an open mind, (b) discard cookie-cutter approaches and (c) make the added effort to learn vital nuances, subtleties and local history. The best national consultants who aim to win do all of this. The snake-oil peddlers who only want a meal ticket don't.

This applies to not only consultants from Washington or Los Angeles who work on campaigns in Des Moines or Mobile, but also to Americans who work overseas, and vice versa.

There are some constituencies that need special care and attention because of their unique cultural diversity and political complexities. New York City, Chicago, Boston, California, Louisiana, Alaska, Hawaii, and parts of Texas and New Jersey, for example, tend to be more difficult for outsiders. Many candidates in these places opt for a heavy presence of local talent on their strategy teams.

In political campaigning, as we have already stressed, one size does not fit all. There's no magic wand, no infallible formula. Each race has its own heart and soul, and must be viewed with particularity and sensitivity. Consultants who understand this reality should never be ruled out just because they're from out of state; but those who don't should be given the boot from the beginning.

The biggest complaints about local consultants – they lack national perspective and access to the best technical talent –

may not always apply, especially if the consultant is experienced in a wide variety of campaigns and has a track record of handling major winning races. It really depends on the consultant's individual credentials.

Ask yourself: Does his or her work stack up to big-name national talent? If so, don't worry about it. If not, maybe you need to look further.

Too much immersion in the local scene may be as much or more of a consultant weakness than too little.

Some local consultants believe they know the politics of their area so well that they assume too much. As such, they fail to explore new themes and test new issues and trends. They tend to typecast local players as "losers" or "winners" and ignore changed circumstances.

Another problem is conflict of interest. For example: Consultant Jones may be a longtime family friend of Candidate Smith, but may find himself or herself working against Smith because of an unavoidable sequence of events. Can you expect Jones to do whatever it takes to beat Smith, somebody he or she will have to live with in the same town for many years to come? If the consultant is a real pro, the answer is yes. Experienced players can separate personal feelings from the requirements of work, just like a good surgeon or lawyer can. But that may not always be the case.

What if Consultant Jones has had a bitter 10-year feud with Candidate Kelly over a private business deal that went bad. If Candidate Smith runs against Kelly and hires Jones, can he reasonably expect that Jones will be objective about Kelly's strengths and weaknesses as a candidate? Perhaps. But maybe not.

These are problems that consultants who only work a local market may have. But these may be problems that have solutions – especially if they're known in advance and everyone takes them into account openly and honestly.

Candidates may ask: Can the fact that I've hired a big-name national consultant be used against me by the opposition? The answer is that if you don't make a big deal about hiring the consultant, and don't parade him or her around your district like a prized peacock, it probably won't ever be effectively used against you, if it's ever used at all.

Voters know candidates hire professionals to run campaigns, just like business people hire lawyers and CPAs to handle specialized legal and tax matters. That's not big news. Just make sure you don't unwittingly make your consultant an issue by excessively relying on him or her for fundraising credibility or by allowing the consultant to speak for the campaign with the local press.

Many times, the questions presented above will be easily answered. If the best local talent is already tied up and not available for your campaign, for instance, you may have to go out of state for professional help, whether you want to or not. On the other hand, if you can't hire the out-of-state consultant you prefer for whatever reason, you may have to make do with a local one.

As in all things, necessity is the mother of invention. In some cases, a *team approach* will give you the best of both worlds: a combination of the best local and national talent.

A campaign may decide, for example, to hire an out-of-state pollster – for national expertise - along with local media consultants – for local expertise.

There are certain venues in the United States that lack adequate local talent. In that instance, you may be forced to go out of town. Even in that case, you may mix national consultant advice with that of a local campaign manager or frequent consultations with smart, loyal, hometown politicians.

This is one problem that is quickly lessening as more and more capable local and regional consultants get into the business and gain rich strategic and technical experience in their areas of specialization.

As strategist James Carville once told me when discussing the political industry: "Some of the best people in this business are local consultants who are completely unknown names on the national scene."

All in all, hiring consultants requires careful thought and honest, open communication. Most of the inherent limitations of out-of-state and local consultants can be compensated for with a balanced team approach that takes advantage of their intrinsic strengths.

Compensating Consultants

Each type of consultant may be compensated in a different way. Here is a quick guide:

1. Media consultants.

Most political media consultants are compensated, in whole or in part, through commissions on advertising buys. As an advertising industry standard, television and radio stations and networks, as well as many newspapers and billboard companies, usually build into the cost of each ad a 15 percent commission. Typically, that commission is given to the agency that places the buy.

Of course, the commission can be negotiated between the campaign and the consultant. In some large campaigns where there are plenty of consultants competing for the business, campaigns attempt to reduce the commissions. However, some media consultants – particularly the most experienced ones who are the highest regarded – will refuse to reduce their commissions.

In addition to media commissions, media consultants may also receive an upfront or monthly retainer fee to cover strategic advice over and above the advertising services they provide. In small campaigns (of budgets of less than $200,000), an upfront fee may amount to $5,000 to $15,000. In larger races, it could go as high as $100,000. In small campaigns, a monthly retainer may range from as low as $1,000 a month to as much as $5,000 a month, depending upon the services rendered. In large campaigns, the retainer may exceed $50,000 a month, again depending upon what services are included.

Out-of-pocket expenses (travel, long distance, shipping, messengers, etc.) are billed extra.

Two very important things to keep in mind:

First, know what the consultant includes as an in-house service that does not require additional compensation or expense. For example, some firms do not bill extra for producer and director services when producing TV ads; others do. That difference may mean many thousands of dollars.

Second, know how the 15 percent commission is computed, and the essential difference between *gross* and *net*. That knowledge could save you a lot of money.

Understand that the 15 percent commission is calculated on the gross cost of the ad. Therefore, if one 30–second spot at the end of a local six o'clock news broadcast costs $1,000, that means the media consultant (or advertising agency that handles the placement of the spot) writes the TV station a check for $850 (which is the *net* amount) and gets to keep the $150 commission payable on that time buy.

Fifteen percent of the *gross* in this case is $150 (15% x $1,000 = $150).

Also, 15 percent of the *gross* produces the same sized commission as does 17.65 percent of the *net* (17.65% x $850 = $150).

Often, ad agencies write into their contracts that they are to get the "industry standard 17.65 percent commission." That's fine, as long as the 17.65 is applied to the *net*, which is the way it is supposed to be. However, if it's applied to the *gross*, which it should not be but in some cases is, then you're unwittingly paying the agency an extra 2.65 percent of the gross amount.

That difference may mean big money.

If, for example, your total media buy is $100,000, the commission should be $15,000, which is 15 percent of the *gross*. But, if an agency charges you 17.65 percent of the *gross*, it will get a commission of $17,650. That's $2,650 more than it is entitled to receive. Of course, if the total buy is $1 million, the difference grows to $26,500, a not insignificant sum.

Basing commissions on net amounts, as opposed to gross amounts, comes in when an advertisement is not commissionable. That means, the price of the ad does not have a commission built into it. So, for an agency to get its "industry standard" commission when it places a noncommissionable ad, it adds 17.65 percent to the *net* amount. Using our six o'clock news spot example, 17.65 percent of the $850 net amount is $150, the appropriate commission.

Most broadcast TV spots are commissionable (meaning that the 15 percent of the gross is included). But some newspapers, radio stations, cable TV and billboard companies sell political ads on a noncommissionable basis.

In some cases, media consultants will charge commissions on other purchases they handle on your behalf, such as printing and media production (studio time, tape editing, lighting, stage sets, graphic design, etc.). When they do, make sure you know whether the commission percentage is based on the *gross* or the *net* amount.

Know the difference. You don't want to leave anything on the table!

2. General consultants.

Most general consultants charge by the hour or by a monthly retainer. Since their primary function is to provide strategic advice and political coordination – not specific deliverables, such as an ad, a poll or a mail piece – this makes sense.

Local general consultants with limited experience may charge as little as $50 an hour, or $1,000 a month. Those with years of varied experience can charge as much as $250 or $300 an hour, or $20,000 a month, depending on how involved he or she will be.

In some cases, general consultants will take a piece of the media commissions either in lieu of retainers or in addition to them. That becomes an issue when one of the general consultant's jobs is to find and interview a media consultant to hire.

Travel and phone expenses are billed extra.

3. Pollsters.

Pollsters provide specific products, namely polls. They can also provide focus group and qualitative interview studies. Usually, they charge set prices for these deliverables.

The cost of a telephone poll is based on two things: the length of the survey questionnaire and the size of the sample. Open-ended questions add cost.

Polls with a sample size of 400 people and 10-minute questionnaires usually range in price from $7,000 to $10,000, depending upon the prestige and experience level of the pollster. An 800 sample with a 30-minute questionnaire can cost between $20,000 and $30,000.

Focus groups of average voters are usually priced at between $3,000 and $5,000 each. Focus groups of harder to reach "elite" or "executive level" respondents (such as corporate CEOs, civic leaders or media executives) may require doubling or tripling these amounts. In fact, certain "elite" focus groups are virtually impossible to do. In those cases, indepth personal interviewing of each respondent is an alternative. Such interviews can be very expensive to get, however.

Pollsters who also serve as ongoing strategy advisers are often paid monthly retainer fees in addition to charging for specific research studies.

Checklist: Questions to Ask

The following questions should be asked of prospective campaign consultants who want your business:

1. When did you go into the political consulting business?

2. How many campaigns have you worked on? What was your specific role in those campaigns?

3. What percentage of your firm's gross revenues comes from political campaigns?

4. What campaigns have you worked on that would be the most like mine?

5. What two or three campaigns do you think were your best, and why? What set them apart?

6. What are your strengths and weaknesses? How would you answer concerns about those weaknesses?

7. Do you only work with candidates from one party?

8. What rule do you follow in terms of working in other campaigns that may pose a strategic or ethical conflict with my campaign?

9. What campaigns will you be working on other than mine? Do you limit the amount of work you'll take on in an election cycle?

10. Please give me three or four references of former clients that I can contact. Please include at least one loser.

11. How are you usually compensated? How is the com-

pensation usually structured? What expenses will you bill me for? Are there any other possible costs?

12. How much time will you, as opposed to your staff members, spend on my campaign?

13. How much of the campaign work will be done by the firm's principals and how much by second and third level staff people?

14. Have you ever been fired from a campaign? If so, why?

15. Have you ever quit a campaign? If so, why?

16. Have you ever been sued because of your political work?

17. Is there anything in your background that may come out and potentially harm our campaign?

18. When are you available to be called, or for meetings? Do you expect to take significant time off for travel or vacation during the campaign? Are you available on weekends and holiday periods for possible calls or meetings?

19. How much control do you want to have in this campaign?

20. If we hire you, when is the deal done and when do you consider yourself committed? Upon signing a contract? Upon a handshake? Upon the first payment made?

21. How do you see the working relationship with the candidate, campaign staffers and other consultants?

22. To what extent will you talk to members of the news media about this campaign, either on or off the record?

23. Will you take or pay any finder's fee or commission, or engage in any fee splitting arrangement, with anyone inside or outside the campaign?

★ Chapter 11

The Power of Targeting

Whether you do it to conserve resources, or to pinpoint individual voters with appropriate messages, targeting is the key to effective voter contact

A sked why he robbed banks, Willie Sutton said, "Because that's where the money is." The same is true when it comes to targeting voters in an election: You go where the votes are. More precisely, you go after the votes you need to win, the ones that are most readily available to you.

Strategically, targeting is based on an age-old military principle: Concentrate your greatest point of strength against the opposition's greatest point of weakness.

When most candidates hear the word "targeting," they think of mysterious computer wizards sitting in Hollywood-style control rooms calculating complicated statistical permutations. It scares them off. As a result, they miss the point of how smart – and basic – voter targeting, combined with good voter lists and database management, can help win over swing voters and save scarce dollars.

Simply put, targeting is the method a campaign – large or small – uses to determine where it's going to concentrate direct contact resources (i.e., mailings, telephone calling, door-to-door canvassing, yard sign efforts, neighborhood parties).

Most campaigns have a limited amount of time, money and volunteers. So they need to make sure that when the trigger is pulled on a campaign activity – whether it's a candidate canvass, a literature drop, a mailing, a round of persuasion calling or a get-out-the-vote (GOTV) door hanger effort – that they reach the right voters with the right messages.

The idea is to use your resources where they will do the most good. Don't spend time or money turning out a voter who is against you; use your resources to turn out a voter who is for you but who needs to be prodded. Also, don't waste your time or money trying to persuade someone who is already either for or against you; use those precious resources on voters who need to be convinced.

That's all targeting is.

If you're a Republican and decide to use the GOTV phone calls you've budgeted reaching only households with at least one Republican registered voter – that's targeting. If you're a Democrat and use your persuasion mail budget on an eight-page tabloid directed at rallying unionized schoolteachers and public employees – that's targeting. If you're a Libertarian or Reform Party candidate and you send out letters announcing your candidacy to the dozen precincts in your district in which Ross Perot and other third parties received over 15 percent of the vote in 1996 – that's targeting.

Even wealthy candidates with unlimited budgets still need to target. For them, it's not so much a matter of conserving resources as it is a need to make sure they're hitting the right voter with the right message. So, in a simple sense, you target for two reasons: *resource efficiency* and *message effectiveness*.

Resource Efficiency

Take an example: If you have 40,000 voters in your district (spread among 23,000 households) and have enough money to send out 60,000 mailers, to whom do you send them?

One approach would be to send *every* individual voter two weeks before election day a persuasion piece (that eats up 40,000). Then, 10 days before election day, send mailers to 10,000 "swing" households that contain registered independents, voters who are determined to be most likely undecided or persuadable. Finally, timed to hit a day or two before the election, send your last 10,000 GOTV mailers to your "favorable" voter list.

There are, of course, other options. Instead of sending 40,000 pieces to every single voter regardless of his or her political affiliation or demographic, you could send five separate mailers to the 10,000 "swing" households. Or, as another option, you could send three mailers to 15,000 "swing" individual voters as opposed to households and then use the remaining 15,000 mailers as a GOTV prod for the 15,000 voters who are most likely to support you.

It's that simple – and complex.

Ideally, you'd send out many more than the 60,000 mail pieces if money were no object. That way, you could do *everything* – persuasion pieces, comparative pieces, GOTV pieces – and then some. But because we live in an imperfect world, with real-life budget constraints, most campaigns are forced to make the hard choices. Setting priorities is what we call targeting for resource efficiency.

Message Effectiveness

Using targeting for message effectiveness is a concept that's easier to grasp. In effect, it's telling voters what they *need* to hear. Telling voters only what they *want* to hear connotes slick deceptiveness. It sounds like you're telling pro-life voters you're pro-life and pro-choice voters you're pro-choice.

Telling voters what they *need* to hear means that a pro-life candidate lets like-minded pro-lifers know that he or she shares their convictions. It may also mean that a pro-life candidate sends an "inoculation" letter to pro-choice voters explaining why abortion should not be the only issue they consider when casting their votes – in effect, reframing the voters' choice around other, more opportune issues.

Targeting for message efficiency is something candidates need to do to win – and it can be done in a way that's entirely honest and philosophically consistent. It is not the same as pandering. It should not connote even a hint of deception.

In campaigns, most targeting is done for both resource efficiency and message effectiveness. When done together, results are maximized.

Four-Step Targeting Process

OK, so now you're wondering: Where do I start? Here's a simple four-step process you can follow:

• *Step One: Develop a profile of your winning coalition.*
Campaigns directed at getting 100 percent of the vote don't usually win, unless of course you're running unopposed. That's because if you try and win over everybody, you're likely not to win over anybody. That's because your opponent will find ways to make stronger, better aimed appeals to voters that he or she may *need* to win than your mushy vote-for-me-because-I'm-for-everything pitch.

Competitive campaigns need to shoot for just enough votes to win, with perhaps a few to spare. They need to figure out who those voters are by studying voting groups that make up the constituency.

No two voters are exactly alike. But over time, voters do behave in ways that can be lumped together into definable clusters. Winning elections is about defining those groups and then stringing together enough of them to give you the total votes you need to win. Building your *minimum winning coalition* (which would be 50-plus percent in a two-way race and perhaps something less in a multi-candidate plurality contest) is an essential part of political strategy and, as we have seen, the message-making process.

In every electoral equation, there are groups of voters (no matter how small or large) who are, to varying degrees, already or potentially favorable and unfavorable to your candidacy. There are also those who have no clear propensities either way.

Good voter file vendors can be enormously helpful in providing the data, analysis and mapping needed for complete targeting programs. Services many of these suppliers and consultants offer are affordable, even for small local and district races.

If you're a first-time state legislative candidate in a primary without an incumbent running, your favorable voter base may consist of your family, friends, work associates and those on your Christmas card or bridge club list who vote in your district. All told, it may amount to a mere 100 or 200 people. But if you're a three-term mayor running for Congress against an incumbent in a general election, you may start with a firm base of over 50,000 favorable voters. Obviously, these numbers vary according to the nature of your candidacy and the size of the electorate.

Decide what your base is, and what it should become. In a general election, for example, this may be a simple matter: Base voters would be those who share your party label. But in a primary or nonpartisan municipal or judicial election, party labels may not be a factor. So you find other variables that matter. When isolating variables relevant to your election, consider the various ways you can slice the population pie:

• *By demography*: Such as voter age, gender, race, income, education and home ownership.

• *By occupation*: Such as white-collar professional, blue-collar, retired, agricultural, homemaker, high-tech, business ownership, military, federal civil service or unemployed.

• *By affiliation*: Such as membership in a political party, the AFL-CIO, the National Rifle Association, the Sierra Club, the Christian Coalition, the Chamber of Commerce, Planned Parenthood, the AARP, Veterans of Foreign Wars, League of Women Voters, a university alumni association, a local civic or garden club, a regional teachers organization, a state medical society or a national trade association.

This may sound like the politics of division. But it's not. It's only divisive if you use the information to make appeals that are meant to tear people apart or to make one sector hate another sector.

Finding population variables that provide a guidepost to people's predictable behavior in elections is as old as elections themselves. It is the way you build a support base, find swing voters and mobilize your vote on election day. Understanding this is the first step to understanding targeting. It is also one of the steps to developing your campaign message (see Chapter 4).

• *Step Two: Identify voters who are favorable, unfavorable and undecided.*

You can do this one or all of three ways:

1. By personal knowledge. The first approach is to collect information on voters through personal knowledge. This is the most precise and personal, yet difficult, way to identify voters. In effect, you enter names of voters you know to be favorable, undecided or unfavorable. They may include friends, family, co-workers, campaign volunteers, contributors, community leaders, rally attendees and people with political signs on their lawns. Regardless of these voters' demographics or affiliations, you know where they stand because you know them.

In the old days of ward politics and precinct organizations, this was the way political machines went after their votes. They knew who they did favors for; they knew who had public jobs; and they knew who their friends and neighbors were. They also knew which voters regularly voted against them.

There's an old story about a powerful ward heeler in Chicago who, on election night, fell into a terrible depression when he got the final vote tally in his best precinct; it was 483 votes for his candidate and seven votes for the opponent. The experienced old pro was dismayed at how the opposition got so many votes. He asked with disgust and shame, "Dammit, I know who those five bastards are, but who the hell are the other two?"

Today, it's harder to know constituents so well. But the more people you know, the more you can identify (ID) as favorable, unfavorable or undecided.

2. By voter ID canvassing. The second approach is to create favorable/unfavorable/undecided voter lists by canvassing voters one by one. Such a program can be very expensive and time-consuming, because it is, in effect, a large-scale poll of your constituency. It is most often carried out through what's termed "voter ID calls," where a professional telephone vendor literally calls each voter or household and asks a series of questions about their attitudes and issue interests. Based on their answers to these questions, each household or individual voter is ranked on a favorability scale.

Of course, this can also be done by volunteer callers or door-to-door canvassers. But it's unlikely volunteers will do the job as quickly or as objectively as will professionals. It is also unlikely that a volunteer phone operation will be able to do the data capture and analysis needed to build a solid database.

Ethically, when voter ID calls are made, the person making the call – whether a campaign volunteer or an employee of a professional phone firm – should explain that the call is being made on behalf of the campaign. Voters shouldn't be told that it is a nonpartisan, confidential survey – because it's not.

Because of the great cost of voter ID programs, they are used sparingly, usually only when and where the less expensive techniques won't suffice.

The economics are simple: Purchasing a voter list with age, party registration and gender may cost as little as 5 or 10 cents a name. If information provided on the list is sufficient to make targeting decisions, you've got a bargain. But calling voters as part of a one-by-one ID program may cost between $1 to $5 per voter reached, depending upon the length of the interview.

Another limitation with a voter ID program is that it doesn't reach everyone. Some voter names do not have telephone numbers attached to them; some names matched with phone numbers won't answer their phones; and some names matched with phone numbers won't talk even if you get them on the line.

Voter ID calls, which provide rich data on the voters they do reach, are best used to supplement other methods by filling in the gaps.

Political consultant Hal Malchow has introduced a sophisticated method to provide for a lower cost alternative to a full voter ID program. He calls it the CHAID (Chi-Square Automatic Interaction Detection) system and first used it in the 1996 Oregon special election for the U.S. Senate.

Instead of calling every voter household in a state or congressional district to identify them as favorable, persuadable or unfavorable, Malchow makes 5,000 to 10,000 ID calls, which is, in effect, a large-sample poll to detect voter leanings by demographic characteristics. The goal of the calls is to create a database of undecided voters.

The CHAID system performs a statistical measurement, predicting at a 95 percent confidence level whether a voter is likely to be undecided or a soft supporter of one of the candidates. A targeting score is assigned to each voter's precinct.

3. Making group assumptions. The third approach is to make assumptions about groups of voters. This is the easiest and quickest way to target favorable/unfavorable/undecided voters because it does not require individual, one-by-one identification. It is, however, the least precise method. For those voters you cannot identify individually, targeting by assumption may be the only way to do it – the method of last resort.

Assumptions may be made based on demography (voter age, gender, race, income, education, etc.), occupation (white collar professional, blue-collar, retired, agricultural, homemaker, etc.) or affiliation (membership in a political party, the AFL-CIO, the National Rifle Association, the Sierra Club, the Christian Coalition, the Chamber of Commerce, Planned Parenthood, etc.).

Voter and other lists can be purchased from public agencies and reputable voter file firms and list brokers. In addition, various group lists – such as club memberships and association rosters – may also be obtained directly from the organizations that maintain them.

• *Step Three: Develop a campaign message and a series of supporting issue points.*

Every political consultant will tell you that every campaign needs a message, a central rationale that communicates to voters why they should pick you over the opposition.

Campaign message-making, as we've already discussed, is based on the theory that the voting decision is a *choice* between alternatives on the ballot. A good campaign message will maximize your candidate's strengths and minimize his or her weaknesses. By doing so, it draws a distinction between your candidacy and the opposition, to clearly frame the choice that voters are being asked to make.

Good campaign messages can be written in one or two sentences. They stress basic themes: It's time for a change; Don't change horses in midstream; past vs. future; liberal vs. conservative; integrity vs. corruption; competence vs. incompetence.

Every campaign conveys a message, whether you intend for it to or not. So you may as well make sure it's the right one.

Veteran political consultant Joe Napolitan once said that all campaigns must first decide what to say and then say it. That's what message politics is all about. Campaigns are about knowing which voters you need to win over and then telling them what they need to know to win them over.

In addition to having a central campaign message, campaigns need targetable sub-messages geared to specific groups. These sub-messages, or issue points, form the basis of a targeted communications strategy.

For example, if a Democratic candidate in an urban area is running on a populist message of "I put people first; my opponent is beholden to the rich and powerful," that candidate could have a set of issue points. One may be geared to African-Americans about the candidate's support for employment programs and minority business development. Another may be directed at union members about support for prevailing-wage legislation and the right of public employees to organize. Another may be targeted to elderly voters about support for nursing homes and senior citizen nutrition programs.

If a Republican candidate in a rural area is running on a conservative message of "I'm against big government and high taxes," that candidate may also have a set of sub-message issue bullets. One such sub-message issue point may be geared to gun owners about the candidate's opposition to gun control. Another may be directed at small-business owners and Chamber of Commerce members about opposition to cumbersome government regulations and the high costs of liability insurance. Another may be targeted to members of

Christian church groups and pro-life activists.

The issue points for both candidates rest on specific themes and policies, but they are all consistent with the central messages of the campaigns. In fact, each reinforces the central message by bringing it home to individual voters.

Issue points may be communicated to targeted voters through any medium that is subject to individualized direct contact, especially mail, phone and door-to-door campaigning.

This brings us to the difference between targeting *by groups* (TV, radio, newspaper) and targeting *by individuals within groups* (mail, phone, canvassing).

In effect, you can target all media, but the precision each medium affords varies greatly. Television, radio and newspaper ads, while effective, are not targetable to individual voters. Some TV shows – especially cable programs – and many radio stations and newspaper zones may be targetable to general population groups (younger voters, women, college graduates, etc.) but not to individuals.

That's why many campaigns use TV, radio and newspaper ads to convey central messages and why they also use mailings, phone canvasses and literature drops to convey individually targetable issue points. In most campaigns, there is ample need to do both.

Remember: Campaign message-making, budgeting and targeting must be considered together, as part of an overall tactical plan; they are "The Three Musketeers" of good political strategy.

• Step Four: Create a voter database.

Over the course of an election, campaigns come across people who are supportive of the cause. It may start with the names of close friends and the family of the candidate. It then branches out to people who sign up along the way.

The favorable voter pool can then be supplemented with expanded lists of friendly groups (local civic improvement associations, trade groups, religious organizations, garden clubs, issue advocates, etc.) and then, based on polling, may also include partisan, demographic and occupational groups within the electorate.

The point here is that every campaign should start from day one building a comprehensive database of supporters.

Think of it this way:

In your campaign headquarters, there are three large boxes: On one box is drawn a smiley face; on another, a question mark; on the third, a frowning face.

Every time someone in the campaign runs across a voter who expresses support, in any number of ways, his or her name and contact information are written on an index card that is thrown into the box with the yellow smiley face.

Every time someone runs across a voter who expresses opposition, his or her card is thrown into the box with the blue frowning face.

All voters who haven't expressed a preference, and who are not members of groups that generally lean one way or the other, are put into the box with the question mark.

Three Boxes

What we have now is the makings of a database of favorable, unfavorable and persuadable voters. This is the heart of targeting. The objective is to watch the box with the smiley face pile up with cards until it is overflowing. Over time, names that are in the box with the question mark should move over to the one with the smiley face.

• The bulk of the campaign's persuasive efforts – those designed to convince undecided voters that you're the best candidate – will be directed to the names in the box with the question mark.

• All of the campaign's volunteer recruitment, fundraising, yard sign solicitation and GOTV operations will be aimed at the box with the smiley face.

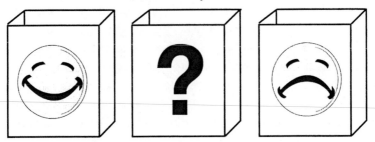

• Names that have fallen into the box with the frowning face will be ignored. (If this is a primary, the names in the box with the frowning face will become quite important as your campaign attempts to bring them over to your side for the runoff or general election.)

In the old days, the basis of a good targeting campaign would literally have been index cards in boxes. Today, computerized database management is light-years more sophisticated. Modern database software does the job swiftly with digital precision.

Scaling the Swings

Now, let's go one step further. Let's divide the names in the box with the question mark into three compartments.

1. *Pushovers* would be undecided voters who are highly likely to ultimately support you once they find out about who you are and where you stand.

For example, if you're a dedicated slow-growth advocate running against a candidate with ties to pro-growth developers, you'd expect that voters who signed an anti-development petition and those who are members of a slow-growth citizens group would ultimately come aboard. The identified slow-growth voters who are not already in your smiley box would be put into the Pushover compartment of the question mark box. At some point, you should be able to move them into the smiley box.

2. *Persuadables* would be undecided voters who have both favorable and unfavorable propensities toward your candidacy. For example: You're running in a primary or a nonpartisan race, and your support base tends to be among older, wealthier voters. However, because you are from the south side of town, and your opponent is from the north side, you don't expect to do nearly as well among voters on the north side as on the south side. So, a 68-year-old voter in an upper-middle-class neighborhood located on the north side would have both favorable (age, income) and unfavorable (geography) characteristics.

The purpose of a campaign is to persuade cross-pressured swing voters to overcome contrary pressures in favor of your candidacy. This may take a multifaceted effort that will include general media (TV, radio, newspaper ads) plus targeted activities (phone, mail, canvassing).

3. *Hard-to-Gets* would be undecided voters who have more unfavorable characteristics than favorable ones.

For example: You do best among union members and young women on the south side of town. Your opponent does best with older, male non-union voters on the north side of town. A 60-year-old businessman who lives on the south side of town starts with three strikes against you (age, gender, non-union) and only one favorable characteristic (geography). Of course, if you can convince this voter that all south siders must stick together regardless of other issues, you may have a shot at him. But it could be a hard sell.

The extent that you devote resources to reaching Hard-to-Gets depends upon how many voters you've identified as Pushovers and Persuadables. If two-thirds of the electorate fall into one of those two categories along with the favorables, you don't have to strain your resources to go after the Hard-to-Gets. But if only 40 percent of the electorate falls within those three groupings, and 15 percent are Hard-to-Gets – who become mathematically essential to crossing the 50 percent line – then you'll have to mount a major effort here.

If you need Hard-to-Gets to reach 50 percent plus one, then by all means concentrate on them. But if you don't need them to meet your coalition goals, you may want to focus more on reaching voters you have determined to be easier to win over (Pushovers and Persuadables).

Where you draw the line between Persuadables and Hard-to-Gets is not an exact science. But wherever you draw the line, it should have at least some rational basis for distinguishing one voter from another. If you don't have any such reason, keep them together in one compartment.

Remember, too, that the number of names in the box with the question mark will relate to the way you budget resources between *persuasion* activities (reaching undecided voters) and *mobilization* activities (getting favorable voters out to vote).

If your district has 50,000 voters and you've put 5,000 in

the box with the smiley face and 5,000 in the box with the frowning face, that means 80 percent of the electorate falls into the box with the question mark. If, on the other hand, you have 20,000 voters in the smiley face box and 20,000 in the frowning face box, you're left with only 20 percent of the electorate in the question mark box. In the former, you'll need a larger budget targeted to voter persuasion. In the latter, you'll need a larger budget targeted to getting favorable voters to the polls on election day.

Ideally, in the end, you will have placed *every* voter into one of these three boxes (with the smiley face box now having more than enough names in it to win the election). Voters are placed in the appropriate boxes based on the three methods we discussed earlier: *by personal knowledge*, *by voter ID calling* and/or *by assumption*.

Assumption is used to identify those voters for whom you have inadequate personal knowledge and who you have not reached with a voter ID contact.

On election day, of course, your entire GOTV operation will concentrate on the names in the smiley box. Your GOTV goal must be to make sure every one of them goes to the polls and votes. As such, you may decide you want to start with favorable voters who have a 50 percent chance to vote (a calculation that can be based on either voting history data, which is available from voter file vendors in many jurisdictions, or through an analysis of other variables that may be good turn out predictors such as age).

For example, you may determine that 25 percent of the voters in your smiley face box voted in at least four of the five past national, state and local elections; 25 percent voted in three of the elections; 20 percent voted in two of the elections; and 20 percent voted in only one of the last five elections; and 10 percent didn't vote at all.

If you only have enough money or time to call half your favorables, you may want to concentrate on the 25 percent who voted three times, the 20 percent who voted twice and one-fifth of the 25 percent (25+20+5 = 50) who voted only once on the premise that those who voted four or five times do not need a turnout prod and those who didn't vote at all or only voted once probably won't vote no matter what you do.

It's like a busy medical emergency room where the overworked doctors devote their time to the patients who need immediate attention to survive, all but ignoring those patients who will live or die no matter how much attention they get.

The same is true for voters. Spend your GOTV resources on those favorables who need it the most.

And to do that right, you need good lists and solid database management throughout your campaign.

From day one of your campaign, always think about those three boxes: What do you want them to look like on election day?

★ Chapter 12

Close Encounters: How to Win Debates

Don't go into a debate with your opponent until you understand the unique dynamics of a face-to-face confrontation

T here was a time when candidates spent countless hours agonizing over whether to debate. The old rule of thumb was that frontrunners had everything to lose by debating, and underdogs had everything to gain. Since most elections have frontrunners, debates were often shunted.

But in recent times, debates have become a fixture of campaigning. Unless you're an incumbent running against only token opposition, debating has become something most candidates can't avoid. Ever since 1984 when incumbent President Ronald Reagan, who enjoyed a big lead in the polls, consented to debate his underdog opponent, Walter Mondale, the incumbent/frontrunner no-show excuse was obliterated.

Now, voters and the news media expect all candidates to debate, whether you're running for town alderman or president. When a candidate won't debate, he or she becomes suspect and subject to attack. Candidates who have good reason not to debate have to weigh the damage done by refusing alongside the risk of doing it.

A 2002 nationwide voter survey conducted for The Pew Charitable Trusts and the Center for American Politics and Citizenship at the University of Maryland found that 57 percent of the respondents would be less likely to vote for a candidate for a major statewide office, and 55 percent of the respondents would be less likely to vote for a candidate for a district or local office, who had refused to debate his or her opponent. By any measure, in any situation, that's a large segment of the electorate to risk offending.

This poll also found that 83 percent of voters believe there should be multiple debates in major statewide elections, such as those for U.S. senator and governor, and that 62 percent believe the same for district and local races, such as those for the U.S. House, state legislature, mayor and county council.

According to the survey, voters like debates because they provide them an opportunity to find out where candidates stand on the issues and how the rivals differ. Voters also say they are more interested in debate substance – the candidates' knowledge and positions on the issues – than style – the candidates' physical appearance and speaking ability. While most voters say they don't care about each combatant's capacity to land attacks on his or her rival, voters do expect the candidates to keep cool and calm throughout the encounter.

Meeting one's opposition in debate can be the scariest thing a political candidate is called upon to do. Experienced campaigners, as well as newcomers, usually get the jitters before they walk on stage to debate. Fear of being surprised with an unexpected attack, or being hit with a question for which you don't know the answer, sets off butterflies in the stomachs of even the toughest combatants. In prep sessions, campaign staff and media consultants should be sensitive to the dread and trepidation with which most candidates approach debates.

It has been said with substantial justification that you don't win debates, you only lose them. Most debate injuries are self-inflicted. That's why careful preparation is critical. However, in your attempt to be careful and prepared, don't become too timid or stiff, either.

It is essential to understand the unique dynamics of a debate. Unlike a regular campaign speech, where you can say whatever you want without fear of immediate rebuttal from your opponent, in a debate you have to be constantly prepared for the comeback – both yours and that of your opponent.

As such, you must think through the arguments you're going to deliver in terms of an interrelated three-part process:

(a) making a point,

(b) anticipating a rebuttal from your opponent and

(c) preparing a response to your opponent's rebuttal.

When presenting your points, rebuttals and responses, make sure they are concise, cogent and clear. Which brings us to another difference between speeches and debates: In debates, you usually have strict time limits. You need to be able to make your points quickly, without hesitation, wasted words or unnecessary pauses.

It's all about preparation, as any good trial lawyer will tell you. Before you walk into a debate: Know what you want to say; think about what your opponent will say; devise answers to all your opponents' claims, both positive and negative.

Preparation, preparation, preparation. If you are prepared, you'll feel prepared. If you feel prepared, you'll have nothing to fear.

Like a boxing match, debates are often scored by pundits and reporters round by round. If your opponent bests you in one round, you have a chance to come back the next round. But always watch out for the KOs!

The following are lessons gleaned by analyzing hundreds of debates over the years among candidates in races small and large, local and national:

1. Determine your strategic endgame before you begin your debate preparations.

The goal of a political debate is not to win the *debate*. It is to win the *election*.

In high school debate clubs, you're interested in scoring the most debating points. But in a campaign, you're interested in winning the most votes, which are usually dependent upon not just the debate but many other factors.

Make sure your debate performance advances your broader campaign agenda. Have a strategic goal when you enter debate preparations. Know what you want to get out of it.

If you're a lopsided frontrunner and do not want the debate to *change the dynamics* of the race, prepare accordingly. That doesn't mean you can't be aggressive or forceful, it just means that you don't want to do anything that will disturb the pre-existing political calculus.

You can be aggressive and forceful without changing the election's dynamics by concentrating on tested themes and messages that reinforce what you've already said.

If your candidacy is a long shot, you may view the debate as the only way to close the gap between you and your opponent. That's the toughest move in the business because – as we've already stressed – debates are more often lost than won. It's tough to perform so well that you can turn around a long shot race in one debate. It has happened, but not often. In addition to a skillful performance on your part, it usually takes a bad showing by your opponent to give you a clean kill.

The biggest debate wins have usually resulted from one candidate's mistakes. Remember how Richard Nixon looked and handled himself during the debate with John Kennedy in 1960. JFK was perceived to be the big winner of the night not so much because of his brilliance but because of Nixon's failures and mistakes.

Rarely will a single debate turn around a race in favor of a candidate – unless the other side screws up. Take the 2000 U.S. Senate campaign in New York between Hillary Clinton and Rick Lazio. The first televised debate between the two candidates was viewed as a turning point in favor of Clinton not so much because of what she did but because of what Lazio did.

Throughout the encounter, Lazio pugnaciously attacked the controversial first lady. The telling moment came when he walked over to Clinton's podium, practically shoved a piece of paper in her face and demanded that she sign a pledge not to allow "soft money" to be spent on her behalf. It was too much. It seemed insulting, bullying. Clinton refused to sign the paper and handled it well. She kept her cool and stuck to her practiced themes and "must air" points. Polls showed that undecided women voters were especially repelled by Lazio's approach. From then on, Clinton gained a sizable lead in most polls and won the race.

Again, it wasn't because of any brilliant move on Hillary Clinton's part that she won the debate politically, it was because of Lazio's self-inflicted injuries.

If you're in a competitive or potentially competitive contest, one in which more than one candidate has a viable chance to win, you may want to use a debate to accomplish one or all of these strategic goals:

(a) Sharpen your campaign's overall message; and/or

(b) Draw clear distinctions between your positions and those of your opponent on select issues; and/or

(c) Address voter skepticism or confusion by demonstrating a personal quality or strength, or inoculating against a perceived personal weakness.

Debates are opportunities to frame the ultimate choice for voters by explaining and illustrating your themes and messages.

For example, when former California Gov. Ronald Reagan debated President Jimmy Carter in 1980, his first task was to demonstrate his own capacity to be a strong national leader and, in so doing, to define a contrast that would be unfavorable to Carter, who was perceived by many voters as being weak and timid. Pre-debate polls showed that a large percentage of the electorate was still skeptical of the 69-year-old ex-actor's ability to protect the peace and to handle the complex duties of the presidency.

Reagan accomplished this first task by the way he handled himself, by the way he looked and by the strength and reasonableness he conveyed.

His second task was to draw out public dissatisfaction with the weakened economy and to turn it full-force against Carter's re-election. He did this repeatedly with specific attacks on a variety of issues. He capped his case with the now-famous line, a killer close that has been copied by hundreds of candidates since then: "Are you better off than you were four years ago?"

It's not likely that your debate performance will be so incredibly good, or that your opponent's will be so incredibly bad, that it alone will win the election for you. Be realistic. Don't try to get more out of a debate than you can reasonably expect.

Debates, by themselves, rarely win elections. But they can nonetheless play a role in a campaign's outcome. Most importantly, they can underscore and reinforce a candidate's strengths or weaknesses. How that relates to what has happened before the debate, and what is to happen after the debate during the rest of the campaign, is what's important.

Don't think of a debate as the dramatic winning play, the decisive Hail Mary pass that single-handedly wins the game. Instead, think of it as one more way to move the ball forward toward the goal line as part of an overall strategy with clear aims and objectives.

2. Know the rules.

A candidate must be fully briefed on the rules of the debate before it begins. That includes knowing the amount of time available for opening and closing statements, answers and rebuttals. It also includes knowing whether and how prepared notes may be used and what visuals (charts, photos, documents, etc.) may be displayed. The rules will directly affect your presentation strategies.

3. Know the physical format.

Your biggest enemy in a debate is surprise.

Do everything possible to reduce the possibility of shock. That includes making sure the candidate is fully aware of the physical format. Whether you will have a podium or table in front of you will affect how you use notes. Whether you will be standing or sitting will influence how you can relate to the opposition.

4. Insist on having a say in the debate format – and think about how it will impact what you do.

Your campaign should always have influence in debate arrangements and should require final approval of the format before you agree to debate. In making format decisions, you will be asked to consider the following:

• Will the candidates stand or sit?

• Will there be a podium or a table?

• How many people can each candidate invite to be part of the audience?

• If televised, who sets up the camera angles and the lights?

• If televised, will reaction shots be allowed? How long will opening and closing statements last?

• What kind of microphones will be used?

• How long will you have to answer questions?

• Who asks the questions?

• Who selects the questioners?

• Will candidates have the right to ask questions of one another?

• When are rebuttals allowed and how long can they be?

• Will surrogates be allowed to represent candidates?

Addressing these issues may have a serious impact on the political consequences of the debate. For example, short candidates may not want to stand near their taller opponents. Contenders who have trouble making a point in quick sound-bites may want an opportunity for longer answers.

A classic case that underscores the importance of this point occurred during the second presidential debate in 1992. This debate was arranged around a town hall format where members of the audience were allowed to directly ask questions. It may have been a tactical error for President Bush, who benefitted from the formality of a podium, to agree to an arrangement which seemed to have better served the interests of challenger Bill Clinton, whose touchy-feely style fit the format.

5. Prepare your opening and closing.

In most debates, candidates are given an allotted time – usually two to five minutes – to open. Don't wing it. Prepare what you're going to say before you walk into the room. Before you open your mouth, know the words that will come out of it.

Your opening will set the stage for the rest of the debate. In laying the foundation for your debate strategy, keep in mind that the opening statement must relate to your campaign's overall message and is one more opportunity to convey that message.

Preparing a close is a little trickier. Although it is important to know how you want to close, and to prepare some closing lines in advance, you also need to remain flexible enough to adjust to the circumstances.

For example, if either you or your opponent stumbles during the debate, you may need to deal with that in your closing. Or, if an opponent levels a serious charge against you and you don't have adequate opportunity to answer it, you may want to use some of your time at the end to do that.

As such, you may want to prepare a three-part "doughnut" close. The first part and the last part of the closing statement will be used no matter what. But the middle part can be jettisoned and replaced with something else more appropriate depending upon what happens in the debate.

If you're given two minutes for a close, you should allocate one minute, half of your total time, to the hole in the doughnut, to the part that can be replaced on the spot. That means the first part can't exceed 30 seconds and the third part can't exceed 30 seconds.

Because it usually takes longer to deliver a statement than you'd expect, perhaps it's best to clip those parts to 20-25 seconds to make sure you have enough time to say everything you must say.

6. Prepare vivid, quotable soundbites for the most difficult and sensitive issues.

Before your first debate, you will probably be able to predict most, if not all, of your opponent's themes and messages as well as questions that might come up. Since debates usually limit statements, answers and responses to 30- to 90-second lengths, you need to have memorable and politically pertinent one-liners prepared. These one-liners can be used to deflect a tough question, handle a sore point or respond to an opponent's attack.

Strategically well-crafted soundbites can get you out of tough spots and help explain complex matters. Most important of all, they provide the quotes that will be published in newspaper stories and rebroadcast on television and radio news shows.

In most downballot campaigns, few voters actually watch or hear candidate debates. But many of them will catch what is broadcast on the news shows that evening or read about them in the newspapers the next morning. Good soundbites – especially those that can be delivered in seven or eight seconds, or less – get coverage. So make sure when you use one that it expresses what you really want to say. Practice the delivery until it's easy off your lips. It may be the only thing most voters see or hear from the debate.

But in the course of this process and preparation, don't allow yourself to become too mechanical in delivering good lines. "Candidates need to think through the points they want to stress and how they're going to say them in a concise, pithy way without sounding formulaic," advises media consultant James Farwell. "It's essential to get across to voters that you actually believe what you're saying and that you really do care about the ideas you're expressing."

Soundbites should be prepared not only to explain yourself and your own issue positions, but also in response to your opponent's expected soundbites and issue arguments.

In 1988, vice presidential candidate Dan Quayle responded to questions about his youth and qualifications with a line that compared his own experience to that of John Kennedy when he was elected president. It was a good line, but it had been overused.

In their televised debate, Quayle's opponent, Lloyd Bentsen, was ready for him. When Quayle popped the Kennedy line, Bentsen came back with the crushing rejoinder: "I knew Jack Kennedy. Jack Kennedy was a friend of mine. And senator, you're no Jack Kennedy."

Another example was the first 1984 presidential debate. Mondale was prepared when Reagan recycled the famous debate line he had used against Jimmy Carter in 1980, "There you go again." In response, Mondale turned the line against Reagan, asking him if he remembered the last time he used the line and reminding him of his own weakness on the issue at hand – in this case, Medicare. Reagan's reaction was uncharacteristically lame and raised serious doubts about his advanced age. Then, in the second debate, when Reagan's age was brought up, he shot back with calculated wit, saying tongue-in-cheek that he would not use "my opponent's youth or inexperience" against him. It was a big hit and in one fell-swoop, it put the age issue to rest.

Presidential candidate George H.W. Bush, in a 1988 debate with Michael Dukakis, responded to one of his rival's mechanical and stilted statements by cracking, "That answer was about as clear as Boston Harbor." It was a perfect debate soundbite: short, funny, pertinent and able to touch upon an embarrassing environmental problem that Dukakis did not clear up as governor of Massachusetts.

In the 1992 presidential debates, independent candidate Ross Perot explained his opposition to the North American Free Trade Agreement by saying that the jobs the U.S. would lose to Mexico as a result of its ratification would create a "giant sucking sound." It was an expression that was colorful and memorable, and one used for years thereafter in discussions about NAFTA.

U.S. Rep. Richard Gephardt, in a debate during the 1988 Democratic presidential primaries, referred to the economic policies of opponent Paul Simon, who had supported some of President Reagan's fiscal plans, as "Reaganomics with a bow tie." Simon's bow ties were a sartorial trademark.

One temptation candidates have when they come up with a good one-liner is to run it into the ground. In most cases, if you sting the opposition with a good hit, let it go. Often, when good lines are repeated too often, they lose their punch.

7. Open the debate on the offense and exhibit cool confidence.

Start off on the offense and stay there. From your first utterance, take the lead, frame the issues, and make your opponent react and dance to your music.

Don't be afraid to be aggressive, or even to attack your rival, if that's consistent with your endgame strategy.

A good opening has as much to do with attitude as it does content.

When working in a close gubernatorial race some years ago, I remember that my candidate – an excellent debater – put a simple sign on his podium that only he could see. It read, "Smile. Cool."

Good advice.

8. *Address the right audience.*

Most political debates are covered by the news media. In bigger elections, many are televised live or rebroadcast. Always remember that the wider news audience is the real audience you're addressing, not the dozens or even hundreds of people who actually attend the debate.

In some cases, the actual live audience may be heavily skewed to certain kinds of voters (students, seniors, liberals, conservatives, business people, teachers, lawyers, etc.) while the wider media audience that will read about the debate in the next day's newspaper or watch soundbites from it on the evening news will represent a much different audience.

Also keep in mind the televised audience. If the debate is being carried only in one part of a state or district, make sure your performance is geared to the political dynamics of that area. But in trying to make targeted appeals, in no case should you say one thing to one audience and something contradictory to another one, regardless of the pressures of the moment to do so.

9. *Get ready for candidate-to-candidate Q&A.*

In many debates and forums, candidates are allowed to ask one another questions. This is an opportunity and a risk. Candidates often wrestle with the choice of whether to ask the opposition a tough, embarrassing question (and risk looking mean) or an easy question (and risk letting the opponent off the hook).

Before you prepare your questions, and possible answers, make sure you know the format and the rules. Usually, the questioner is given a chance to respond to the answer. If that's the case, drop your bomb in the response, not in the question. Make sure you set a trap for your opponent, and then close the trap in the comeback. Try to get your opponent to talk about something that you can smash in your response. But if, as a questioner, you can't comment on the answer, make sure your question is asked with that limitation in mind.

10. Prepare for all possible questions, even easy and light-hearted ones.

In most elections, candidates are asked the same dozen questions, over and over. Candidates should never, ever walk into a debate without being prepared to handle at least those questions. They should also be prepared to handle variations of them.

In addition, also prepare for simple, funny, or off-beat questions, such as:
- Why are you running for this job?
- Can you say something nice about your opponent?
- What's your biggest flaw or weakness?
- What's your biggest asset or strength?
- Who is your political hero?
- What's your favorite book? Movie? TV show? College football team?
- What book are you now reading?
- How often do you go to church?
- What charities do you support?
- If you could be an animal, what would it be?
- If you could be a tree, what would it be?
- What's the price of a loaf of bread? A gallon of gasoline? A gallon of milk?

These may seem irrelevant or trivial, but prepare answers for them anyway.

The problem with cute, off-beat questions is surprise. And as we know, surprise isn't a good thing.

Two examples come to mind.

When U.S. Rep. Ron Wyden was running for the U.S. Senate in Oregon, he was handed a world globe and asked to find certain countries in the news, such as Bosnia. He was unable to do so. Later, he explained that he couldn't see map details without his glasses. A reasonable enough explanation, but he didn't say that during the debate. He looked befuddled, embarrassed. Of course, his opponent ran TV spots with the clip of his globe fumbling. Flunking the geography test probably hurt Wyden's standing, but he won a close race anyway.

During the 2000 race for the Republican presidential nomination, the candidates were asked to name their favorite political philosopher. Frontrunner George W. Bush answered, "Jesus Christ." Other candidates in the debate, as well as many pundits, said they didn't consider Christ a *political* philosopher. Nonetheless, Bush held his ground. Some voters liked his answer, especially Christian conservatives – an important GOP primary bloc. Others saw it as odd and even as blatant pandering to a key voter segment.

Both the Wyden and Bush examples show how twists on unexpected questions in a debate can have an impact.

Make sure that when a surprise question hits you, you don't look like a deer caught in headlights. Use of wit can also be extremely effective as long as it isn't corny, silly or mean-spirited.

11. Talk to the audience, not your opponent.

As a general rule, you should address yourself to the audience – to the voters. The classic example of this was the first 1960 Kennedy-Nixon debate, in which Nixon seemed weak and insecure largely because he kept addressing Kennedy, as if he were trying to get his opponent's approbation, instead of reaching the millions of voters viewing him on TV.

Voters don't want to watch politicians bicker. They want to be talked to directly.

There are exceptions, of course. Occasionally, you may need to address your opponent when you make a point, ask a question or answer an attack. However, depending upon the format, these should be rare occasions.

12. Surprise the opposition.

Remember: Your opponent is as scared as you are. The

last thing you want is to be surprised, to be thrown off stride. Conversely, do something early to rattle your opponent, whether it's a new attack, raising a previously untouched issue or displaying documentation. Attitude can be a powerful weapon. Walk into the room where the debate is being held with an air of ease and confidence. You may be able to surprise your opponent by how cool, polite and in control you are.

13. Know the difference between two-candidate and multi-candidate debates.

In a multi-candidate forum, it is usually important to figure out a way for your candidate to stand out from the crowd, to make a singular impression. Some candidates have attempted to stand apart through the positions they have taken on issues or by attacking their opponents. Others have tried physical gestures, like the time Bruce Babbitt stood up and challenged his opponents for the 1988 Democratic presidential nomination to stand with him in his admission that new taxes would be needed to reduce the deficit.

The dynamic of a multi-candidate debate can be considerably different from a two-way match-up.

Two rules to remember:

• First, if two of your opponents are fighting between themselves, let them have at it. It will behoove you to hold their coats while they slug it out. It gives you a chance to rise above the fray. Also, watch for an opening when you can sweep in as the great statesman and clean up their mess with a well-placed bon mot.

• Second, if you get into a two-way verbal contest with one of your lesser adversaries, and there's no way to easily extricate yourself from it, quickly drag your major opponent into it. Don't let him or her off the hook.

A major issue when there are more than two candidates in a race is which ones will be allowed to debate. It is usually to the disadvantage of an incumbent or a frontrunner to have too many opponents on stage. On the other hand, if you're stuck with them, it's unwise to appear as if you don't want them there. Remember how George H.W. Bush looked in 1980 when he and Ronald "I paid for this microphone" Reagan were tussling over who would be included in a New Hampshire debate?

In the past, it's proven crucial for third party candidates to be included in debates with the major party candidates. Ross Perot was included in the 1992 debates and it was essential to his impressive showing of 19 percent of the vote. Four years later, Perot was not included, and his vote percentage fell to 7 percent.

Wrestler Jesse Ventura, who ran as a Reform Party candidate for governor of Minnesota in 1998, was a clear underdog when he was allowed to join his Democratic and Republican opponents in televised debates. His performance in the debates, and his ability to stay out of the crossfire of attacks and counterattacks that flew between his two opponents, allowed him to stand above the fray.

In the case of Ventura, his major party opponents ignored him and concentrated their fire on one another. That was probably a big mistake and demonstrates how you have to weigh the seriousness of a so-called "minor" candidate before you ignore him or her.

The Minnesota debates gave underdog Ventura, an imposing physical presence, a chance to show how he was a sensible alternative to two bickering, partisan politicians. Of course, Ventura went on to win the three-way race. When preparing their debate strategies, his opponents should have viewed him as a major threat, not as a minor nuisance.

14. Be careful when leveling an unprepared attack.

If you're going to attack the opposition in a debate, make sure you're on sound footing and have thorough documentation. Avoid cheap shots and retain a sense of personal dignity and overall fairness.

Often, candidates are tempted to respond to a surprise attack by hitting their opponent with a broadside that has *not* been thought through or lacks proper evidence to support the claim. Be careful.

As media consultant Michael Sheehan advises his clients, always stop short of where you're tempted to go when making an unprepared attack.

Don't paint yourself into a verbal corner that you can't escape. Nothing looks worse than taking a jab at your opponent and then being forced to either back down from it or to split hairs over what you really meant to say.

15. Avoid fighting with the debate moderator or panelists.

For the most part candidates look mean and petty when they get into a fight with a debate moderator or with a panelist. Remember, you're not running against them no matter how much they may irritate you. Sometimes, however, if a moderator or panelist goes too far in something they say or skirts the rules to the opposition's clear advantage, it may become necessary to point that out in a way that doesn't look too priggish. If you make such a challenge, keep in mind how it will look to the viewing audience, so avoid being obnoxious, annoying or pedantic.

Haggling over debate rules and making excuses why you can't properly get your point across doesn't communicate well to a mass audience. That mistake was made by Perot in his 1993 debate with Al Gore over NAFTA, in which Gore was rated the clear winner.

Debates are hand-to-hand combat. They involve a complex set of rules, strategic pitfalls and tactical opportunities. You need to be ready.

Woody Allen once said that 80 percent of life is just showing up. That's not so with debates. With them, 20 percent is showing up and 80 percent is preparation.

★ Chapter 13

The Picture Perfect Image

Every candidate needs five really good photos

Good - make that great - candidate photographs are essential components of any campaign, from a small local race to a large statewide election. In political campaigns, pictures can be literally worth a thousand votes - or more.

Considerable attention, time and - unfortunately - money must be devoted to make sure that candidate photos convey the right image and message. Once, when I was a political media consultant, I used $3,000 of a total campaign budget of $30,000 in a local school board campaign for black and white photos. The candidate thought I was nuts - spending a sizable 10 percent of her overall war chest on pictures! But there was method to the madness.

In this campaign, which was on behalf of an unknown challenger against a controversial incumbent, we only had enough money for two direct mail pieces, a handcard, yard signs and one week of radio. Consequently, everything had to be just right. Even though my candidate went door to door every day for over two months, she was destined to meet only about 20 percent of the voters in person. The other 80 percent of the electorate would know her by her pictures - only.

Another point: My candidate was the mother of three beautiful young daughters, all of whom were public school students. So it was crucial that she be presented as a smart, caring mother with a strong stake in the success of the educational system. The photos were terrific. They could have been magazine cover shots. And they did the job. On election day, we won the race.

The lesson of the story is to do whatever is necessary to get great photos. Don't skimp. Hire a first-rate photographer with experience doing either news or fashion formats, preferably both. Get a professional stylist to do make-up and advise on appearance. Also ask the photographer to bring adequate lighting equipment for both indoor and outdoor shots.

One critical thing to remember is that the photographer needs to shoot a lot of pictures, literally hundreds of exposures. Many photographers, particularly those who specialize in studio portraits or weddings, will want to shoot two or three rolls of 24 or 36 exposures and leave it at that. But insist on more.

A photographer needs to shoot 50-100 exposures of each of the five poses described below to make sure he or she gets the right picture in each category. Many of them will resist doing this much shooting, and a few may even try to scare you with talk of high processing costs for so much film, but make them keep clicking.

If you're going to the expense of paying a photographer, a stylist and a lighting person a full- or half-day rate, make sure you get a large enough selection of shots.

In every campaign, there are five basic pictures a candidate needs. With these images, you can define the complete candidate, as a person and as a potential public official.

Furthermore, you can use these photos in your TV spots as well as in all of your print materials (mailers, brochures, tabloids, cards, fliers, newspaper ads, posters, billboards and possibly yard signs).

The five essential shots are:

1. The Portrait Shot.

You will need a straightforward, full-faced pose that can be given to newspapers and a variety of club bulletins and newsletters. Often, publications will want a simple, formal portrait with a neutral (preferably dark) background. Should you smile or look serious in this shot? The answer is that you want a pleasant expression on your face, which could mean a slight smile. But it depends upon the kind of image you want to project.

If you want to project the look of a serious-minded, mature public leader, perhaps grinning broadly is not a good idea. If you want to portray a more friendly, neighborly image, then a smile may be in order.

2. The Picture-That-Says-Everything Shot.

You will need a photo that says everything about the candidate you want to project, whether it's honesty, warmth, sincerity, intelligence, energy, wisdom, experience or compassion. In many cases, the Portrait Shot is so good, it can be used for this one, too.

Unlike the Portrait Shot, this picture can be a profile or a three-quarters profile. It may show the candidate smiling, even laughing. In the case of a mom running for the school board, it may show her reading to her kids. For other situations, it could show the candidate making a speech or in physical movement.

3. The People Shot.

Candidates must also be photographed surrounded by average people, shown relating to them in a populist way. Being in public office means you have to know how to deal with people, how to communicate with them and how to listen to them.

Voters want to see how a candidate looks relating to others. Whether you're a liberal champion of the disadvantaged or a conservative, pro-business advocate, you'll need a strong people shot.

The key to this photo is to shoot it tight. Have a variety of people (dressed like they're on their way to the mall) packed around the candidate.

There shouldn't be much blank space people between; nearly the whole frame should be filled by humanity. There should be a friendly, natural atmosphere.

Watch what the candidate is doing as he or she is relating to others. Even though there may be six to 10 people in the scene, the focal point is the candidate's expression.

4. The On-The-Job Shot.

Show the candidate at work on something that relates to the office being sought. If you're running for a judgeship, this may entail sitting in a law library reading through case-books. If you're running for sheriff, you may want to be shown in a law enforcement scene talking on a walkie-talkie. If you're running for an executive position, you may want to be seated at a large desk while talking on the telephone. If you're running for a legislative post, you may want to be seen at a podium. Voters want to have some idea of what you look like when you're working. Do you look like a congressman? A mayor? A governor? A county commissoner? A judge?

5. The Family Shot.

If the candidate has a spouse and children, this is an important photo.

If the candidate isn't married or doesn't have children, this shot may not be possible. Although you can often substitute parents, siblings, grandparents, cousins, aunts and uncles for spouses and children, doing so usually produces a result with less effect.

The Family Shot must always be casual and should project a smiling family with a happy home life.

Never dress up for this photo. You don't want to look like you're putting on airs. Wear casual, neat, ordinary clothing. The key to this picture is the expression on the faces of the family members.

If a spouse looks uncomfortable or unhappy, that will send out a very negative message. If a child looks despondent or discontented, it will ruin the whole image.

Rest assured voters will focus on these details. So have the photographer expose a lot of film on this one.

In addition to these five pictures, you may also need specialized shots with seniors, children, farmers, plant workers, police officers or teachers. Some campaigns will need pictures on location, showing the candidate at a certain school, hospital, park or river. These location shots may be useful when producing literature targeted to specific voter groups.

Big campaigns require a file of numerous photos. Every

campaign, no matter how small or large, needs basic shots to fully define the candidate.

Got the picture?

★ Chapter 14

Slogans That Sell

Finding catchy, potent phrases to communicate your campaign's message

A campaign slogan is like a soufflé. A good one rises to perfection. A bad one falls like a stone off a ledge. Take Ronald Reagan's re-election theme in 1984: "Leadership That's Working." Simple, easy to understand and on target, this catch phrase succinctly summarized what many Americans already believed – that Reagan, in contrast to his predecessor, was a strong leader who had made things better at home and abroad.

For bad slogans, consider Barry Goldwater's 1964 motto "In Your Heart You Know He's Right." Sounds fine, but for someone who was fighting an image as a right-wing extremist, the inevitable play on words was a net loss. Opponents countered with, "In Your Guts You Know He's Nuts."

Slogans force campaigns to define themselves in a short statement consisting of simple and clear language. They crystallize a candidate's strengths, draw contrasts with opponents and illustrate in concise soundbites complex, substantive campaign messages.

"Good slogans have rhyme, rhythm, or alliteration to make them memorable," writes columnist William Safire. "Great slogans may have none of these, but touch a chord of memory, release pent-up hatreds, or stir men's better natures."

A campaign slogan should not be confused with a campaign message. In modern politics, a message positions a candidacy and provides a central rationale as to why the candidate is the right one at the right time, preferable to the alternatives. A slogan, on the other hand, is a shorthand way to explain and illustrate to the public the various aspects of the campaign's message.

Slogans have been around a long time. The Oxford English Dictionary traces them back to 1513. Slogan styles have varied with the temper of the times. "Tippecanoe and Tyler, too" was one of the earliest presidential campaign mottos. It spotlighted William Henry Harrison's victory at the Battle of Tippecanoe in 1811 and was notable because it's one of the few that even acknowledged the existence of a vice presidential nominee.

Highest Form of Flattery

Like old soldiers, winning slogans never die. In fact, they rarely fade away. In literature, it's called plagiarism; in politics, it's called experience. For example, when Harrison's grandson, Benjamin, ran for the presidency in 1888, he dusted off the old man's winning line and used it again. "Tippecanoe and Morton, too" may not ring quite as loudly in the ear of history as did the earlier version, but it was ultimately as effective. Benjamin Harrison won his race, too.

Candidates have to be careful which slogan they purloin, however Patrick Buchanan, when running for the 1992 Republican presidential nomination, used the theme "America First." These words, on face value, seem about as safe as you can get. But Buchanan's enemies drew unflattering comparisons between his slogan and the same one that had been used a half-century earlier by the "America First" committee, an isolationist group that opposed U.S. entry into World War II.

Over time, slogans became more issue-oriented. In 1856, voters were treated to: "Free Speech. Free Press. Free Soil. Free Men. Fremont and Victory." Here, John C. Fremont unabashedly laid out a platform as well as a catchy lyric.

In 1896, William Jennings Bryan's slogan had nothing to do with either his name or his background, but instead was directed at his issue: free silver. "16 to 1" was the Democratic battle cry, underlining Bryan's populist proposal to increase the money supply by coining 16 ounces of silver for each ounce of gold. Republican William McKinley took the opposite stance: "In Gold We Trust" and "Sound Money."

McKinley also campaigned on the theme of "A Full Dinner Pail" – an attractive promise for workers and families struggling through the Industrial Revolution.

Perhaps the most unpretentious issue-oriented slogan was the one used by a local candidate in Washington, D.C.: "Dog Litter – An Issue You Can't Sidestep."

Liabilities Into Strengths

Crafting campaign messages that turn a candidate's liabilities into assets is nothing new. Ulysses Grant may not have been an illustrious president, but his image as a military victor was vital to his appeal in 1868. His rallying cry "Let Us Have Peace" was the strategic equivalent of a home run. It sent an important signal that a general-as-president wouldn't necessarily plunge the nation into another bloody conflict.

Campaign themes are also designed to reassure voters. This can be a risky tack, however, when the adage centers on a weakness in your own candidacy. The perfect example was Woodrow Wilson's desperate 1916 campaign that hinged on his ability to maintain the peace. "He Kept Us Out of War" was his theme. It was phrased retrospectively, as a statement of fact, and not a promise for the future. There was no explicit vow that, if re-elected, Wilson would continue to keep the country out of war, but only a declaration of the obvious that, up to that point, he had kept America out of war. Crafty old Woody had pulled a fast one. Only months after his re-election, America was very much in the war.

Some slogans are time bombs. If America had entered the world war before election day, Wilson's campaign pitch would have been a mockery. Any campaign theme that can be undermined by uncontrollable events is a gamble. Nelson Rockefeller's assertion in 1968 that he was "The One Republican Who Can Win in November" was shattered when poll results on the eve of the GOP convention showed Richard Nixon running better against the prospective Democratic nominee than Rockefeller was.

Occasionally, slogans miss the strategic mark and end up hurting the candidate they're designed to promote. Standing for re-election in 1932, hapless Herbert Hoover wrapped himself in the status quo and asked voters to "Be Safe With Hoover" – right in the middle of the Great Depression! When Birch Bayh used "It Takes a Good Politician to Make a Good President" in the 1976 New Hampshire presidential primary, it fell flat. Watergate era voters wanted nothing to do with traditional politicians, good or otherwise.

Most large campaigns have more than one slogan. Eisenhower used "I like Ike" on buttons and banners, but his central theme "It's Time for a Change" packed the strategic punch. Lyndon Johnson's 1964 campaign – arguably the first modern media-age presidential campaign – used "Let Us Continue," asking voters to carry on with John Kennedy's unfinished agenda, as well as "All the Way with LBJ" and "LBJ for the U.S.A." as rhymes used in songs and on signs. "Vote for President Johnson on November 3. The Stakes are Too High for You to Stay Home." was the TV spot tag line, a get-out-the-vote pitch that was important because only a very low and skewed election day turnout could have eliminated Johnson's large lead.

George Wallace always came up with solid slogans for his losing presidential bids. In 1968, "Stand Up for America" shifted attention from his racial politics toward a more uplifting, patriotic theme. "Send Them a Message" was the perfect pitch for a protest candidate to use in the 1972 presidential primaries. Four years later, Jimmy Carter successfully countered him with "Send Them a President."

Ins and Outs

For "outs," most slogans center on change. When voters are ready to oust an incumbent regime, it's a tough theme to beat.

There are many ways to phrase the change message. In 1946, Republicans asked the question, "Had Enough?" In 1960, Kennedy used "Let's get this country moving again!" In 1968, Hubert Humphrey found himself cast as the candidate of an unpopular status quo. To remind voters of his long record of legislative accomplishment, his campaign made the case that "Some Men Talk Change. Others Cause It." In 1976, Carter and Walter Mondale tied concepts of change and leadership together and came up with "Leaders, for a Change." In 1980, Reagan focused on the incumbent's economic and international misfortunes as a backdrop for "Let's Make America Great Again."

During the 1992 presidential primaries, Democratic candidates tried to one-up each other on the change issue. Bill Clinton talked about his "crusade for change" and cast himself as "The Change We Need." Tom Harkin proposed to "Build a New America." Nebraska Sen. Bob Kerrey started with "Fight back, America" and then settled on "Courage for a Change." Former Massachusetts Sen. Paul Tsongas went even further, calling himself "The Big Change."

Change isn't always the magic word. It can be an unacceptable path when the "ins" are popular. America did not want change in 1936; they wanted FDR and his New Deal to "Carry On," just as they wanted the Kennedy-Johnson prosperity in 1964, and Reagan's "Morning in America" in 1984 to continue. Often, the stay-the-course theme has an added dimension. "Connecticut Works Better Because Ella Works Harder" was Gov. Grasso's way of linking job performance to visible improvements.

Experience is a central focus of many re-election slogans. Lines like "Keep (candidate's name) On the Job" or "Keep (candidate's name) Working For You" have decorated signs and brochures for incumbents from dog-catcher to governor. "Experience Makes the Difference" was Nelson Rockefeller's theme in 1970 (in addition to the unadorned but potent "Governor Rockefeller for Governor") and "Experience Counts" was used by Vice President Nixon against the less experienced Kennedy in 1960. "Re-elect the President" and "Now More Than Ever" were Nixon's successful re-election slogans in 1972.

On occasion, geographic identifications are apt, such as Gov. Martha Layne Collins' "Experience Counts, Kentucky" and Martin Schreiber's "Experience Makes Wisconsin Work." In running for re-election as governor of Kansas, John Carlin based his message on the notion that "Running for office is one thing. Running the office is something else." In 1986, Gov. Michael Dukakis told his state's voters

"Massachusetts is in good hands," Gov. Madeleine Kunin explained her rationale for another term with the phrase "Results for Vermont," and Sen. Tom Daschle characterized himself as "South Dakota's Best."

Sharp Contrasts

Along with experience, other personal qualities have been used as slogans. Words such as honest, integrity, qualified, fair and tough have called out from billboards and bumper stickers across America.

Sometimes, these words don't fit the candidate or the situation and are merely empty rhetoric. Using "integrity" presents a sharp contrast if your opponent is under federal indictment for bribery, but may not mean much when personal trust isn't an issue. One campaign that did use its candidate's personal qualities effectively was produced by consultant Dan Payne for Detroit's mayor: "Strength. Experience. Pride. The Right Stuff. Coleman Young. The Mayor." Another viable slogan strategy has been "Common Sense – Uncommon Courage," a theme used by Sens. Henry "Scoop" Jackson and Phil Gramm, as well as many others.

Possibly the best incumbent "mea culpa" came from New York's telegenic Mayor John Lindsay in his rough-and-tumble 1969 re-election. Lindsay's flaws were too well-known to hide. So hometown media consultant David Garth came up with a theme that didn't even mention what Lindsay had done or promised to do as mayor. It simply said: "It's the second toughest job in America." The implication: Being mayor of this ungovernable city is so difficult, don't expect anybody to do it very well. It did the job. Lindsay won a second term.

Ironically, one of Lindsay's city hall successors, Ed Koch, was elected in 1977 on the theme, "After eight years of charisma *[a shot at Lindsay]* and four years of the club house *[a swipe at incumbent Mayor Abe Beame]*, why not try competence?" The author of that provocative line was none other than David Garth, the man who had previously sold the eight years of charisma to the Big Apple.

Some slogans accent the sound of a name. To clarify an

unusual surname spelling, William Greenhalgh, a candidate for county executive in Maryland, once used these rhymes: "Get On the Balgh With Greenhalgh" and "This Falgh, Vote Greenhalgh."

To rhyme with the unexpected pronunciation of his name, Congressman Bill Schuette entreated voters to keep him "on duty." The closing line of a television documentary for unsuccessful Virginia gubernatorial candidate William Battle was fitting and powerful: "A Man Worthy of His Name: Battle."

After his defeat as a presidential candidate in 1964, and his retirement from the Senate that same year, Barry Goldwater made a sentimental comeback in his home state in 1968 when he regained a Senate seat with this slogan: "Senator Barry Goldwater. Doesn't that sound great?"

Your slogan, suggests media consultant James Farwell, "should say something about who you really are and what you really are. Some slogans sound great, but if they don't fit your candidacy or personality, they'll boomerang and give your opponent an opening to attack your credibility."

Populist Appeals

Many slogans associate candidates with average voters. "People First" was particularly effective in Bill Clinton's race against George Bush largely because Bush was viewed as being out of touch with ordinary folks. Dukakis' last-minute pitch in 1988 that he was "On Your Side" was a populist appeal many observers thought he should have developed much earlier. A 2000 Senate candidate in Michigan used, "Debbie Stabenow: On our side."

Hubert Humphrey was fond of calling himself "The People's Democrat." Texas Sen. Ralph Yarborough's re-election theme "He fights the people's fights. And he wins." stressed not only populism but effectiveness. More recently, a North Carolina trial lawyer won his 1998 race with the slo-gan: "John Edwards: The people's senator."

Getting things done is a common theme for office-hold-ers. Messages crafted by Garth for U.S. Rep. Richard Ottinger's U.S. Senate campaign and U.S. Rep. Hugh

Carey's gubernatorial campaign in New York are good TV-age examples. "It's easy to promise. It's a lot tougher to deliver. Ottinger delivers." was a successful pitch that won Ottinger his party's nomination even though he ultimately lost the general election.

"This year, before they tell you what they want to do, make them show you what they've done" was Carey's way of making the point that political promises should be viewed in the context of a track record. It worked and Carey won. Nearly a quarter century later, Delaware Sen. Joe Biden won his re-election bid with a familiar: "Before they tell you what they'll do, make them show you what they've done."

Presumptuous, open-ended slogans are delicate. When you say a candidate "has done a lot" or ask voters to "look at the record," you're inviting the opposition to turn these words on their head. "Senator Smith says he's done a lot. Let's look at what he's done. He voted against pensions for police widows. Then he voted to raise his own pay." Make sure a clever line isn't too clever by half. The one thing worse than running against your opponent is running against yourself.

Candidates with controversial records or philosophies slightly to the left or right of mainstream often run as "fighters." John Tunney, son of a famous boxer, won a California Senate seat by asking voters to "Put a fighter in your corner." Frank Bellotti's earthy gubernatorial theme was "Massachusetts is worth fighting for." Incumbents have frequently used the generic "(candidate's name) Fights For Us." One candidate, who wanted to make sure he was seen as a battler for what's right, claimed he knew "how to fight, who to fight and what to fight for." "He'll make your fights his fights" is a popular line that combines a fighter-populist image.

In 1998, Republican Sen. Don Nickles used: "He's there every day, fighting for Oklahoma." That same year, Sen. John McCain's re-election TV campaign in Arizona hailed its candidate for, "The character to do what's right and the courage to fight for it." McCain carried through on these themes in his unsuccessful 2000 race for the GOP presidential nomination. But Sen. John Kerry of Massachusetts, a decorated Vietnam veteran like McCain, had used a similar theme two years before the Arizonan did: "Courage, principle, leadership: John Kerry, fighting for us." Sen. Mike DeWine won re-election with, "A proven fighter for Ohio's kids and families."

Sometimes, though, fighting isn't enough. John Lindsay's failed 1972 presidential bid used the argument, "While Washington's been talking about our problems, John Lindsay's been fighting them." Given his poor showing in that race, voters apparently wanted a president who would do more than fight problems; perhaps they wanted someone who would solve them. Maybe that's why a Louisiana businessman running for the U.S. Senate told voters in 1996, "The politicians offer excuses. Bill Linder finds solutions."

The Unslogan

Slogans can stress what a candidate is not. "Unbought and unbossed" was Shirley Chisholm's banner. "Not just another politician" has been fashionable for newcomers running against established politicos.

As electronic media began to dominate electioneering, so did slogan creativity. "Let's do something about the state we're in" was the piquant double-entendre consultant Joe Napolitan used for underdog Senate winner Mike Gravel in Alaska. "Joe Tydings never ducks the tough ones" was used by an incumbent senator from Maryland who had cast a number of liberal votes out of step with his more conservative constituents. (Tydings was defeated by Glenn "You know where he stands" Beal.) "He's for real. The quiet man nobody owns, everybody respects," was successful for William Winter's gubernatorial run in Mississippi, largely because it was true.

In 1998, Sen. Pat Leahy of Vermont identified himself with his state's image: "A different kind of state. A different kind of senator."

Classic examples of hip slogans were the two used in the late '60s by New York Senate candidate, Paul O'Dwyer: "He doesn't cop out" and "Elect a man who gives a damn." These tough-talking, down-and-dirty phrases seemed daring at the time, but now appear to be relics of a Tom Wolfe narrative about Manhattan's radical chic.

Gender references in campaign slogans have also undergone a transformation. As recently as a few years ago, candidates were still calling themselves "the man for the job" or "the right man for Cincinnati." One city council candidate ran on the slogan, "Let a man do a man's job." Apparently, nobody in that 1969 election ever asked why male testosterone was considered to be the most important qualification for a city council seat. Don't expect to see many slogans like that anymore.

On the other hand, women are often elected on themes that emphasize gender as a symbol of change, honesty or independence. "She's not just one of the boys" was a common slogan for women running for office in the late '70s and throughout the '80s. "Put the state's purse strings in the hands of a woman" was another.

In recent years, slogans have often been crafted as tag lines for television spots.

Democratic gubernatorial candidate Gray Davis of California, facing two multimillionaires in the 1998 primary (one of whom poured over $40 million of his own money into his campaign), ended his TV spots with the zinger: "Experience money can't buy." And he won.

Two years later, across the country in New Jersey, Democratic Senate candidate Jon Corzine, who spent $63 million – $60 million of which was his own money – to win his seat, had a battery of ads with alternating tag lines. "Standing with us. Fighting for us. Jon Corzine: Our values in the Senate" was one of them. Another was, "Bold ideas. New answers. Jon Corzine."

A similar theme was that employed by losing Democratic Senate candidate Brian Schweitzer of Montana in 2000, who ended his ads with: "Plain talk. Good ideas."

Sen. Joe Lieberman of Connecticut, the 2000 Democratic vice presidential nominee, simultaneously ran for re-election to the Senate that year. To play off of his newfound national stature, he used: "Joe Lieberman: Making Connecticut proud." His GOP Senate opponent countered with a down-home approach that tried to subtly remind voters that their senator was off campaigning everywhere but Connecticut with: "Phil Giordano for Senate: Putting Connecticut first." State pride is a frequent formula. Maryland gubernatorial candidate Ellen Sauerbrey offered in 1998, "The integrity and independence to put Maryland first." Unfortunately for her, voters that year put her second.

Values have become increasingly important in campaign messages. Sen. Ben Nighthorse Campbell's 1998 re-election slogan was, "Values, independence, courage for Colorado." In 2000, a former governor running for the U.S. Senate successfully used: "George Allen: Leadership and Virginia values."

In the end, candor is perhaps the most endearing quality in any political slogan. The 1991 gubernatorial runoff in Louisiana pitted racial extremist David Duke against Edwin Edwards, a much-investigated ex-governor with a well-earned reputation for Las Vegas high-rolling. Many unhappy voters were confounded by what they saw as a choice between a "Nazi" and a "crook." To address this dilemma, an Edwards supporter came up with this masterpiece: "Vote for the Crook, It's Important."

Now, there's a reason to go vote if there ever was one.

★ Chapter 15

Controlling the Agenda

What to do when outside advocacy groups and political party committees run their own campaigns while you're trying to run yours

Once upon a time, elections were about people who wanted to get elected to public office. It was a fairly simple concept. But now, there are new contestants in the campaign ring. Interest groups and political party committees are running their own campaigns – separate and apart from those of the candidates. This is especially true in major congressional and statewide elections that have national implications and in key state legislative races that may determine party control.

Independent campaigns usually center on issues that the sponsoring organization wishes to promote and, by so doing, seek to help candidates who agree and harm those who don't. They are the "x-factor" of modern political strategy that, according to GOP strategist Whit Ayres, gives "almost everybody involved in campaigns heartburn at one time or another."

Traditional notions of issue advocacy – public campaigns aimed at influencing legislative and governmental decision-makers – differ from this new brand of electoral advocacy, which is aimed at influencing *voters* during an election. Of course, many of the groups that pioneered issue advocacy and grassroots lobbying – regulated industries, organized labor, trial lawyers, environmentalists, term limit advocates, pro-life and pro-choice activists, to name the majors – are now mounting expensive, sophisticated, high-profile campaigns that are designed to elect and defeat candidates on election day.

After watching what happened in elections beginning in 1998, and carried through in 2000 and beyond, candidates and political consultants see the handwriting on the wall and fear this expanding intrusion on candidate campaigns. In fact, their growing fear of being hit by friendly fire is almost as great as their dread of attack.

"It's a very disconcerting trend," says pollster Ed Goeas, president of The Tarrance Group. "I think we'll reach a point in the future where you may see the bulk of the campaign being run from outside of [candidate] campaigns in terms of developing the messages, delivering the messages and determining what the messages are."

As more private sector organizations learn to use the tools of the political campaign industry, a broad range of corporations, associations, unions and nonprofits are playing a larger, more aggressive role in shaping public opinion on matters they deem important.

This phenomenon – together with an overflowing political money supply that has washed away the make-shift dams of campaign finance regulations – is rapidly cutting new channels of cash that flow through interest groups instead of candidates. A study conducted by the Annenberg Public Policy Center of the University of Pennsylvania estimated that during the 1995-96 election cycle one-third of the total dollars spent on advertising in federal elections was attributable to "issue" advocacy efforts.

Given the trend, it is no surprise that many observers blame it on the backfiring of campaign "reforms" (such as contribution caps and, in some cases where permitted, spending limits) that were enacted in the 1970s and were supposed to reduce the importance of money in politics. "All of this is an unintended consequence of the most convoluted system of campaign finance laws imaginable," says Ayres, who believes the current system of regulations "ought to be junked, scrapped and thrown out."

Losing Control

Whether or not the laws are changed, the patterns of the

recent past – more interest groups running wider interference in more candidate elections – are here to stay.

"Candidates are losing control of their own campaigns," observes Democratic analyst Mark Mellman. "We have independent groups that decide what the message is going to be, decide what the timing is going to be .... It is a very uncomfortable position to be in."

Consultant Jim Duffy, a Democratic media consultant, echoes Mellman's thoughts: "As candidates lose control and as advocacy groups take over, candidates become props in campaigns."

Goeas, an adviser to top Republican Party leaders, sees this type of campaigning continuing.

The man who directed polling for President Clinton's re-election says the trend has intensified because of vast social and economic changes. "We are in the middle of a communications revolution," posits Democrat Mark Penn.

"We have seen the [television] networks fundamentally broken as the main communications vehicle ... the Internet growing at an astounding rate ... the balkanization of interest groups and issues ... If you project out, we're going to be looking at a totally different political communications system" in the future, surmises Penn. "Independent groups and little niches of people are probably going to become much more important."

Define the Terms

Welcome to the brave new world of politics.

It is such a changing world, in fact, that we don't even have meaningful words to describe it. Terms of art like *independent expenditure, issue advocacy* and *soft money* are often confused and used interchangeably. Let's look at the differences:

• An *independent expenditure* (called an "IE") is a political activity paid for by individuals, interest groups and, since a 1996 Supreme Court ruling, party committees, to influence an election that cannot be constitutionally prohibited because of First Amendment rights. The catch is that an independent expenditure must be an arms-length transaction. It cannot be made in cooperation or coordination with the candidate's campaign it is intended to help. Federal campaign finance law changes enacted in 2002 placed restrictions on many of these expenditures which, of course, provoked lawsuits to test the ability of Congress to regulate IEs.

IEs were, in effect, created by a 1976 Supreme Court ruling (*Buckley vs. Valeo*) that declared legal limits could be placed on campaign *contributions* but not on campaign *spending*; it is a distinction that many reformers have criticized. Nevertheless, IEs that expressly advocate the election and defeat of candidates have been considered by the courts as expressions of free speech outside the control of many statutory restrictions.

• *Issue advocacy* is the promotion of policy viewpoints through advertising, public relations, voter education and grassroots mobilization, often with tax exempt funds. The materials and ads usually avoid asking voters to directly vote for or against anybody. They usually attempt not to "expressly advocate" a candidate's election or defeat to stay outside legal donation limits.

• *Soft money* is the term used to describe a contribution given to a political party by a group or individual that is supposed to be used to finance party-building activities (such as administrative overhead, volunteer recruitment, voter registration and get-out-the-vote drives).

As long as soft money was used only for its intended purpose – i.e., legitimate party-building – it was not much of a factor nor was there a powerful incentive for most givers to give. But beginning in the 1990s, the parties used soft money to fund media, mail and phone operations that serve the specific purposes of their candidates' campaigns. Astonishingly, from a legal viewpoint, they got away with it.

Because soft money was not supposed to fund federal candidate campaigns, it was not subject to the limits imposed on federal candidate contributions for individuals and for PACs. It was also not restricted as to its source, which means corporations prohibited by law from contributing directly to federal candidates can donate to party soft money accounts. Under the provisions of the 2002 campaign finance law passed by Congress, soft money would no longer be available to federal-level party committees and would become a function of state and local party committees with new restrictions on contribution size and use.

To the extent these three vehicles of involvement relate to candidate elections, we can call the entirety of the activities these terms describe *indirect campaigning.*

Escalating Costs

There are pragmatic reasons more groups are using indirect campaigning: first, and most obviously, to get around low contribution limits; second, to exercise greater message control over the communications they fund; and third, to exercise greater control over who spends their money.

The escalating costs of political participation, driven largely by expensive new technologies, have enticed big players to devise ways around contribution limits. In an age when many U.S. Senate contenders spend over $10 million and U.S. House candidates often shell out over a million dollars just to be competitive, $1,000, $2,000 and $5,000 contributions seem like mere drops in the proverbial bucket. Today, if you want to alter the outcome of an election, you need to spend tens of thousands of dollars – maybe even hundreds of thousands or millions – per election.

Interest groups with a controversial issue agenda are finding that the only way they can introduce their issues into the public dialogue of most campaigns is to do it themselves and not to rely upon candidates – even friendly ones – to do it.

Democratic media consultant Brad Lawrence says these groups "get a two-for-one" in that "they not only advocate for or against a candidate, they also get to advocate and advance their issue." If they just donate money to a candidate, who can then spend it however he or she chooses, they "only get one."

"Organizations are realizing that to push their agendas they need to control how it is being pushed. Once they give money to a campaign, they've lost control over how it's spent and what it buys," adds Lawrence, a principal in New Jersey-based Message & Media Inc.

An added reason for the propagation of indirect campaigning is money control. If a group gives a candidate money, or gets its members to give money through its PAC, then the candidate controls the spending. That means the candidate's media people, pollsters, mail and phone vendors get all the fees. But if the group spends the money itself, it decides who gets the business. It's old-style patronage, only here it's not public jobs being dispensed but private contracts.

Conceding that many outside groups are more comfortable with their own consultants, Lawrence says it is the state parties that usually care more about who the consultants are than the interest groups. The latter tend to concern themselves more with the content of issue messages, he maintains.

Money control is closely tied to message control, argues Duffy, and is not so much "consultant-driven as it is interest group-driven." He says, "The consultants are not pushing this as much as the group leaders who are fighting to preserve their niche and the identity of their issues."

Quicker On Your Feet

Love it or hate it, indirect campaigning can throw a candidate's plans into a tailspin. It influences the pace of electioneering, the intensity of media buys, the timing of attacks and counterattacks, and the direction of issue spin.

"We're going to have to be quicker on our feet as operatives, as planners," says Alan Secrest, president of Cooper & Secrest, a Democratic polling firm. "Your antennae are going to have to be that much better. You're going to have to be that much farther ahead of the curve whether through research, or through word of mouth or through your own experience."

Consultants and managers, counsels Secrest, need to learn to be more disciplined "in terms of the job you do on behalf of your candidates ... in introducing yourself and sometimes in introducing your opponent as well."

Message discipline isn't always easy to maintain, warns Secrest, because "oftentimes we don't know where that third party money is going to come from and where it's going to land." In addition, he advises candidates to consider starting earlier with larger media buys and greater spot repetition so they can get their "message through before some of these distractions come into place."

Former GOP media consultant Ann Husted reinforces Secrest's point: "The best way for candidates to protect themselves is to set the agenda and tone of what you want your campaign to be about before outside groups come in."

Husted's former employer, Brabender Cox Mihalke, handled the media for conservative activist Gary Bauer's Campaign for Working Families in the 1998 special congressional election in the 22nd District of California on behalf of GOP primary winner and general election loser Tom Bordonaro. This race, which was an Olympian tournament for indirect campaigners of both the left and the right, strengthened her belief that candidates need to "go out and raise more early money" so they have the "firepower to get their message out" – from start to finish – regardless of outside interference.

Strategists have found that substantial voter confusion over the sponsorship of political messages is created when groups other than the candidates are running ads. Average voters watching their TV sets or listening to the radio or reading mail pieces and newspaper ads don't always catch the tiny disclaimers or discern the subtle differences between a candidate-sponsored communication and an independent group-sponsored communication. "The distinction is almost irrelevant as far as voters go," says Lawrence.

The Dirty Work

It is typically easier for an outside group or party committee, whose name is not on the ballot, to take the strategic risk of sponsoring a slashing attack than it is for a candidate to do so. It's no wonder, then, that much indirect campaigning is negative.

A content analysis of political materials in the 1996 presidential race conducted by the Annenberg Center found that "issue" ads were 41.1 percent negative as compared with the candidates' ads, which were 24.3 percent negative.

There may be, however, another side to the coin. If outsiders do "the dirty work," will that reduce the pressure on candidates to attack their rivals?

Not necessarily, say many pros. "Smart campaigns won't let it affect them. They'll still have to rise or fall based on their own communicative ability," advises Duffy. "You can't rely on a special interest to do your work. If you do, you're making a serious mistake because the work may never get done or it may never get done right."

GOP media consultant Jim Innocenzi, of Sandler-Innocenzi, similarly counsels clients that it's "a risky strategy for a candidate not to lay down the contrast between you and your opponent in hope that someone else will do it."

But Cleveland, Ohio-based Democrat Bill Burges has a somewhat different take. Though he believes outsider attacks may eventually reduce the burden on candidates of going negative, he says the real impact will be on the tone and style of candidate-sponsored ads, which may have to be crafted as exclamation points to the group-sponsored attacks. Strategist Burges says candidate ads should consider using more humor in their spots to underline what third parties have already said.

How to handle outside attacks is a big tactical issue for consultants and candidates. Husted suggests that to solve this tricky puzzle, campaigns must first determine whether they have "the resources to keep their own agenda out there" no matter what else is happening. That must be the first priority, she insists. Then campaigns must "determine whether responding will move them off message and onto an issue they don't want to fight over." But in some cases, she acknowledges, if the attack is big and harmful enough "you may have to deal with it regardless."

Some media pros liken group attacks to those that come from an opposing candidate: "You have to respond," asserts Innocenzi, "you can't sit there and hope nobody's paying attention."

One approach is for the victim to vilify the attacker. That's a strategy that media consultant Scott Howell says was effective for then-U.S. Rep. Tom Coburn when the Oklahoma Republican's re-election candidacy came under a barrage of negative media sponsored by the AFL-CIO.

"We made big labor and the union bosses the bad guys and then we tied them to [our Democratic opponent] Glen Johnson," says Howell, whose ads urged voters to call Johnson's office and "tell him to stop the lies the union bosses are spreading about Tom Coburn."

Adds Howell: "It worked so well, Johnson's negatives went up to the point that labor pulled out of the district in the closing days and redirected their resources to more promising contests."

Another strategic danger for candidates is that of friendly fire.

What if an outside group's ads inadvertently miss the intended target and accidentally hit the candidate they are intended to help? This is a troubling prospect for any candidate caught in a triangulated assault.

When both enemies and allies conspire, albeit out of far different motivations, to place you smack in the middle of an issue battle you'd just as soon not fight, you may easily find yourself in an impossible strategic "pincer" with no way out.

For example, if you're a candidate and don't want to make abortion an issue, you may be forced to face an opponent's abortion attack from one direction and a "friendly" abortion group's attack against your opponent from another direction – trapping you into a corner that threatens to shift your focus away from more favorable issue contrasts.

When boosters launch a hard-hitting attack backed up by a saturation media buy, no one can be absolutely sure what it will accomplish or how the opposition candidate will respond. Outsider messages – more than candidate messages – have greater potential to boomerang, points out Duffy, because the groups sponsoring them "don't always have the benefit of watching how the campaign is progressing day to day. They may not be as sensitive to local issues and concerns as the candidate's campaign team."

Burges notes that only a few years ago many of his clients wished that "somebody would come in from the outside and drop $50,000 on their behalf." But now, he says, they're scared; they don't want anybody, friend or foe, to knock them off message or to overwhelm their message.

Another problem may be the uneven quality of advertising produced by independent groups that are not well-versed in the subtleties and nuances of political campaigning. "Some of it is smart, some stupid," says Innocenzi, who is particularly critical of production techniques, labeling many creative treatments "absolutely awful."

Complaints about misguided and poorly executed friendly fire are often heard from moderate Democrats, particularly in the South, who fear that AFL-CIO-sponsored attacks against their GOP opponents buttress Republican attempts to paint them as "pawns of big labor" even when their philosophies and records may tilt otherwise.

Republican candidates have a similar worry: Indirect campaigning by hard-line conservative organizations may make it easier for Democratic opponents to portray them as "right wing extremists" even if that portrayal does not square with the candidate's own pronouncements.

Of course, not all candidates decry outside assistance. Says one recent congressional candidate, "In our race, supportive groups did things we could never do, like get a lot of out-of-state money and air very tough ads that we'd never try on our own."

Beauty, here, is in the eye of the newly elected officeholder – the person who will ultimately decide who gets credit for helping and who gets blame for thwarting.

Improper Reflections

The implications of indirect campaigning run deeper than the purely tactical. Although advocates believe it benefits democracy by enhancing the discussion of issues – especially the kind of controversial matters that candidates usually want to avoid – others, from both sides of the aisle, view the trend less favorably.

Laments Duffy: "Regardless of which side you're on, whether you're helped or hurt, you can't see what's happening as a good thing. Treating candidates as a mere pass-through diminishes the process."

Diminishing candidates in the electoral process, it could also be argued, subsequently diminishes their capacity for leadership in the governmental process.

"Campaigns are supposed to be a reflection of candidates," says Mellman. But "if the campaigns are controlled by outside groups who ostensibly have never met, have no idea about and no coordination with those candidates, then those campaigns are not proper reflections of those candidates."

The implications of crowding the political field with outside players are far-reaching and go to the heart of voter participation. In the end, concludes Mellman, this trend makes "it harder – not easier – for people to make judgments about the choices they want in elections."

And all that makes being a candidate a harder job.

★ Chapter 16

Re-Election Tips for Legislators

Winning the next election begins the day after you won the last one

An overwhelming majority of legislators – federal, state and local – are re-elected every election. Lawmakers who are defeated are usually those who are embroiled in scandal, reapportioned into an unfavorable new district or perceived to have lost touch with their constituents. There's not much that can be done about a scandal or a reapportionment once the deed is done, but the third risk is one that every incumbent needs to guard against.

The best way to prepare for re-election is to immediately focus upon a plan of action to keep you in close touch with the voters. The following nine tips will go a long way to accomplishing that goal:

1. Keep your perspective.

The world looks different from behind the high marble walls and big bronze doors of the state capitol or city hall. Smart incumbents, especially in swing districts and states, need to keep that in mind as they delve into the minutiae of legislation.

Insiders may think in terms of bills, resolutions and amendments, but voters think in terms of problems and solutions. Although administrative bureaucrats, committee staffers, professional lobbyists and colleagues from both parties are all vitally important to your role as a legislator, don't forget that these people – no matter how knowledgeable or powerful – are highly unrepresentative of the electorate that sent you there.

If you forget the folks back home, they may return the favor on election day the next time around.

2. Speak the right language.

If you want to communicate with most English-speaking people, you don't say it in Russian. If you want to get something across to German-speaking people, you don't tell it to them in Chinese.

The same is true about legislative dialect. Language used in the lawmaking process – just like language used in courtrooms or in operating rooms – is foreign to outsiders.

So, if you want to communicate with your constituents, directly or through the press, talk to them in a language they understand – and that ain't Legislativese.

New legislators, federal and state, are prone to becoming so impressed with themselves as they learn insider lingo that they can't wait to show it off. Beware of that, because it happens slowly and naturally. Though an occasional use of a technical term may be OK, make sure you always couple it with everyday language.

For example, when doing media interviews and making speeches at home, avoid excessive use of bill numbers and committee names and stay away from bureaucratic words like "finalize," "establish" and "supplemental." Instead, use terms like "end," "start" and "extra."

3. Immediately after- your election, quickly create an impression that you're reaching out to your constituents and keeping your promises.

First impressions are critically important to voters and news reporters. Early efforts that show you're working overtime to stay in contact with the people of your district or state will quickly establish a highly favorable – and enduring – image that will serve you well for your entire career.

Once you're perceived as an effective, tireless, in-touch legislator, it'll be extremely difficult for a future challenger to destroy that impression.

Here's a useful tip: The first time you go back home after you've been sworn in, make a big deal over it. Arrange numerous meetings with supporters, talk to the press, hold town meetings, send streams of mail. Your first visit home is a window of opportunity that doesn't last long, maybe only a few weeks. So do it right. It'll create a first impression that will last forever.

4. Don't forget your friends.

Go home with the one who brought you. Translation: Keep your political base happy.

This doesn't mean you have to give every interest group that supported you everything they want – they'll often overreach and ask for more than they'll expect you to give them – but it does mean keeping bonds of friendship and trust strong and lines of communication open.

This requires a two-pronged strategy: First, stay in touch with the organizational leadership of your support base both at the capitol and city hall (lobbyists) and at home (association officers, citizen activists, local PAC directors). Consider them part of your political family. Keep in touch. Ask their advice on a range of issues, even those that may not be on their agenda. Don't mislead or lie to friends in a sneaky effort to curry favor with the other side; they'll catch you as sure as the day is long – and then you'll be left without friends or respect.

Second, make direct appeals to the grassroots base of friendly constituencies. Don't just talk to the leaders. Communicate with their membership – through mailers, invitations, questionnaires – and let them know that you're looking out for them. This ensures that cross-pressured voters who have multiple affiliations – the Chamber of Commerce AND the NRA; the Women's Political Caucus AND the Sierra Club – relate to your overall approach to representation above and beyond your voting record on a single issue.

5. Reach out to political opponents.

After getting elected, some politicians can't wait to cut out their opponents. Doing so may make you feel good temporarily, but it can also solidify a base of opposition that, if allowed to fester and grow, could ultimately kill you.

The wisest course is to go to your political opponents after the election is over and let them know that you're respectful of their views – even when contrary to your own – and will work with them in a cooperative way. In fact, go further and ask them for their ideas; let them know you're sincere about wanting to include them.

Of course, this doesn't mean you should put your enemies above your friends or sell out your principles. Stick to your guns – and your base – in terms of policy and the casting of roll call votes. But as you do, be careful how you treat the people on the other side. Don't add insult to injury.

Be kind and civil to people who supported your opponent in the last election. Let them know that you will make a real effort to find out what they think and attempt to find common ground that affords them real input.

6. Send out newsletters that solicit citizen views.

Don't just tell your constituents what you think, ask them their opinions. Use your newsletters not just to disseminate information but to seek it.

In preparing a survey questionnaire for citizens, make sure the questions are not so slanted and biased that it will frustrate or needlessly offend them.

Once you get the returned questionnaires, immediately send each citizen a thank you letter for responding. Keep track of the issues they raised in their surveys, put the information in a database and as legislative action is taken, write to them about what you're doing.

Make it clear on the front page of your newsletter that you're sending this mailing to keep in touch with voters – the way you promised you would do.

Also, put your newsletter on the Internet and use the Web to seek voter views and to provide helpful information about various public services and government agencies.

7. Hold town hall meetings.

Voters like access. Town hall meetings provide a popular vehicle for public interaction.

Town hall meetings should be promoted through your newsletter as well as local press outlets. A good format for a town hall meeting is to open with a 15- to 20-minute "report to the people" summarizing recent news and to give your views on the issues of the day. If there is a particularly important matter of concern to the public – i.e., the construction of a new highway or the closing of a nearby military base – you may want to have people from the relevant agencies on hand to provide background and to answer technical questions. You may also want to develop a format that gives each side a chance to have a say.

After the initial presentation, it should be opened to questions. But before you ask for audience questions, make it clear that you will stay after the public meeting to handle individual or private questions.

The key is to be a good listener. Make it clear from the outset that you respect every point of view expressed and will take each citizen's input seriously. "You may not always agree with me on every detail on every issue, but at least I listen, at least I'm open-minded and at least I'll tell you straight where I stand" – that should be your motto.

You can also put your town meeting on a local cable TV channel and run ads in the TV section of the local newspaper promoting the programs. Of course, keep in mind that if you allow a telecast of the meeting, it provides a videotaped record of any gaffes or mistakes you make that could find their way into the hands of future opponents.

After the meeting, send each attendee a thank you letter.

8. Build a really good database.

You should keep an active database of all the registered voters in your constituency. The list should include every piece of information legally available: address, phone number, e-mail address, party identification, age, issue interests, group membership and political involvement. Newly registered voters should be added on a monthly basis and should be sent a letter welcoming them into your area.

Voters who were identified as being favorable or unfavorable in your last campaign should be entered into the database. Volunteers, contributors, sign locations, issue activists and interest group affiliations should also be entered. As voters call or write you, note that contact on the master list; as they express their views on issues – pro or con – keep track of that, too.

If you maintain your database carefully and always enhance it with new information, you will have a powerful grassroots contact tool when it comes to re-election time.

Of course, be careful that you don't improperly use public property to build and maintain this data bank. Play it safe. Don't risk getting into trouble.

It may be tempting to use free government facilities and equipment at your disposal to conduct political activities, but don't fall into that trap. Many elected officials have crossed the line and paid a dear price for their indiscretions.

9. Rebuild your press relations.

You believe that some reporters treated you unfairly at least a time or two in your last campaign. But once you're elected, the best thing to do about those slights – however painful and harmful they may have been – is to forget about them.

Start fresh. Make it clear to reporters, editors, news directors and publishers that you're going to be accessible to them and treat them as professionals doing a job.

You want to have a reputation among the news media as being open and accessible. Let reporters know that you're not only a quote source but a good, honest clearinghouse of governmental and legislative information.

10. Communicate with new voters.

On a monthly basis, collect the names and addresses of all new voters in your district. This includes names of those who are registering the first time as well as people who have moved into your area.

Once you have the contact information, contact them. Welcome them to the voter rolls from your district. Send them a questionnaire seeking their views. Let them know how to contact you as well as other relevant public agencies. Give them your Web site address so they can keep up with what you're doing for them. And, above all, add them to your database for future contact and follow-up.

Some districts, especially those in high-growth areas, change dramatically during a term of office. Stay on top of those changes – that is, if you want to keep winning.

★ Chapter 17

Handy Tips for the Campaign Trail

How to stay focused, put your best foot forward and survive the day by day grind

The following tips, suggestions and bits of advice are offered to provide practical guidance for your campaign days:

Keeping Your Eye on the Ball

• **Don't let the bastards get you down.** Every day, you'll hear bad news. If it's something you need to deal with, deal with it instantly. If you can't do anything about it, then forget about it. Candidates have a lot of bad days. Expect them, and move on.

• **Always keep your cool.** Campaigns run on chaos and unexpected events. Don't let them throw you off your message and game plan.

• **The goal of being a candidate is winning the election.** It's not to indulge your ego, to make people like you or to get even with your enemies. Aim to get more votes than the opposition. Nothing more. Nothing less.

Bill Clinton was such an effective candidate because he understood that he always had to keep his eye on the prize. He knew his goal as a candidate was not to get voters to trust, like or even to respect him. His goal was to get them to *vote* for him. In his 1996 re-election race, when he recited accomplishments of his administration, he'd often say something like, "Don't trust me, look at what (so and so) said." Or, "You

204

don't have to take my word on this, a study by (some reputable organization) came up with these numbers." Clinton knew many voters didn't believe or trust him. But trust was not what he really wanted. Votes were what he really wanted. So he didn't indulge his ego by trying to get voters to believe or trust him. He knew he could win votes from people who were wary of him personally but who thought he was doing a good job. So he didn't push it; he simply said what he had to say to get the votes. Period. Nothing more. Nothing less.

• **No matter how hard you try, you won't get every vote that's cast and you won't get everybody to like you.** That's true with every politician, even the most popular and best loved. So figure out what votes you need, and go get them. Elections aren't popularity contests.

• **If you want a political career, don't let defeat stop you.** Instead, learn from defeat and apply the lessons to your next campaign. Some of the most successful politicians have suffered stinging defeats along the way.

Abraham Lincoln lost his first election, for the Illinois state legislature. Before he won the presidency in 1860, he suffered two U.S. Senate defeats.

Franklin Roosevelt lost the Democratic nomination for the U.S. Senate in New York by a landslide in 1914 and six years later lost the vice presidency by a landslide while running on the ticket headed by Gov. James Cox of Ohio. Shortly thereafter, he contracted polio and was paralyzed from the waist down. But that didn't keep him from rebuilding his political career. In 1928, he was elected governor of New York and in 1932, president. He won re-election to the White House an unprecedented three times.

After a meteoric six-year rise from young veteran to member of Congress to U.S. senator to vice president, Richard Nixon lost the presidency in 1960 by a razor-thin margin. Two years later, he lost the governorship of California and, in a bitter morning-after press conference, made his famous "you won't have Nixon to kick around anymore" comment. Six years after that humiliation, he was elected president.

Before Ronald Reagan won the 1980 GOP presidential nomination, he had lost two prior attempts, in 1968 and 1976.

George H.W. Bush lost two U.S. Senate races in Texas and one Republican presidential nomination bid, in 1980, before he was elected vice president and then president.

Bill Clinton lost his first race, for Congress. He went on to get elected state attorney general and then governor. But then he blew his first gubernatorial re-election campaign in Arkansas. That didn't stop him, however. After being out of office for a term, he came back, and won the governorship back from the man who had beat him.

George W. Bush, like Clinton, lost his first race for Congress. Eighteen years later, he sought the Texas governorship, and won it. Only six years after that victory, his first, he was elected president.

These presidents of the United States could have let defeat destroy them, but didn't. Instead, they picked themselves up, started over and won the ultimate prize in the business.

Moral of the story: Don't give up when you lose. There is always another day, another election, another set of opportunities.

Dealing with the Voters

• **Ask voters for "help" as opposed to "support" or "votes."** Help sounds less political, more personal and it's harder for someone to respond in the negative.

• **Ask *every* voter for help.** Don't miss anybody. That includes waiters, parking lot attendants, bus boys, janitors, your next door neighbor, your dentist, your child's soccer coach and the bank teller where you cash your checks.

• **Listen.** Don't just shake your head as if you're hearing what people are saying when, in fact, you could care less. *Really* listen. The best one-on-one politicians are those who, when you meet them, seem as if they've tuned out every-

206

thing and everybody else and are focused on you like a laser beam.

• **Beware the huge contribution.** Don't ever take a campaign contribution that's so large that you won't be able to return it if the donor ever asks you for something while you're in public office that you can't do for him or her.

• **Say thanks.** Whether it's just expressing gratitude, or writing personal thank you notes, always show appreciation for help and courtesies. President George Bush, the elder, was known for the handwritten thank you notes he constantly wrote to acquaintances and supporters. Over the years, those notes accumulated into large numbers, and they became a big part of his success.

• **When someone tells you they're voting for your opponent, don't get mad.** Don't lash back, no matter how rude or nasty they are. Candidates filled with anger and hatred look like losers.

• **Don't skimp on television production just to put a few extra dollars on time buys.** Candidates tend to be biased against spending money on spot production in favor of spending more on time. When presented with a $75,000 TV budget, most candidates would instinctively rather allocate $5,000 to spot production and $70,000 to time buys than to allocate $10,000 for spot production and $65,000 to time buys. But in many cases, that is a mistake.

Some TV spots can be produced for very small budgets (under $3,000). But in some situations, a much larger budget is required to ensure the quality needed to pull off a good ad concept. On-location shooting, computer animation, online editing, lighting, music, voice-overs, film stock are all expensive; and the more complicated the spot, the more it costs.

Before you argue down your media consultant's production budget, ask yourself this simple question: Would you rather spend $70,000 airing a mediocre spot or $65,000 airing a really effective one?

Doing Media Interviews

• **Don't view the news media as the enemy.** A negative attitude toward reporters will ultimately do you more harm than good. If you can't develop a thick skin, you can't be in the game.

• **Don't be afraid of the press.** They will sense it and assume you're hiding something. Be accessible and be honest with them.

• **Look them in the eye.** When being interviewed by a TV reporter in a stand-up setting, look at the interviewer and not at the camera. When being interviewed in a TV studio with the interviewer in the same room, look at the interviewer, not at the camera. When being interviewed in a TV studio, and you're alone in the room (the interviewer and perhaps other guests are elsewhere), look into the camera. Keep your eye contact steady, even when others are speaking.

• **When being interviewed on TV, and you're seated in a deep, soft, cushy chair or sofa, sit up straight and lean forward some.** You may have to position yourself fairly close to the front of the seat to do this. Don't lay back in the chair, or don't sprawl out on the sofa, like you're home watching your favorite TV show – it'll look sloppy.

• **In a taped TV interview, make sure you express complete thoughts in quotable soundbites of less than nine seconds.** Anything longer probably won't make the evening news.

• **The press communicates news with headlines and interesting quotes.** They don't cover extended or complicated arguments.

• **Prepare soundbites.** Before you do a media interview, develop one, two or three readily quotable soundbites that succinctly express what you want to communicate to voters – regardless of the questions.

After the 2002 California gubernatorial primaries were over, Democratic nominee Gov. Gray Davis did a round of media interviews discussing the upcoming general election campaign against opponent Bill Simon, a GOP businessman. Davis, a past-master of the packaged soundbite, was quoted in a newspaper article describing his rival as "out of touch and out of sync with most voters" because "he is pro-life, pro-gun, pro-voucher and pro-deregulation."

In a nationally televised interview the same day, Davis repeated nearly identical phraseology that he had used to attack Simon in the newspaper quote, and added a soundbite about where he stood in contrast to his opponent: "I am proudly pro-choice. I signed the toughest gun safety laws in America. And I solved, as best any governor can, this crazy deregulation scheme I inherited."

These concise statements were geared to getting quoted in newspaper stories and were carefully designed as soundbites that would fit perfectly into an edited television or radio newscast.

• **If you know a reporter is going to ask you a question about something you'd rather not talk much about, start your answer with a short "bridge" statement that addresses the question but then quickly gets you to what you'd prefer to talk about.** In one campaign, my candidate was running against an incumbent state senator who had been convicted on a business fraud charge. The incumbent said it was a partisan inspired prosecution and pledged to appeal the legality of the jury's verdict.

The press badly wanted to embroil my candidate into the controversies surrounding the trial. I didn't. We were ahead, and our campaign was doing well concentrating on positive issues such as crime, education and streets. The only way the incumbent could win was if he and the press were able to turn his criminal case into a partisan matter and make it a campaign issue.

My candidate and I prepared a "bridge" soundbite for him

to use every time a question was asked that related to the court case. It was, "The facts are the facts." By saying this simple phrase, my candidate was able to dismiss the matter without talking about it and, more importantly, to get the interview on to more favorable territory.

"The facts are the facts," he'd say, and then continued, "but the issue in this campaign is who can do a better job representing the people of our district, fighting against crime, fixing streets and working for better schools."

My candidate never allowed the press to bait him into making any remarks about his opponent's legal problems other than the simple "bridge" soundbite. It worked – he won in a landslide.

• **Never say "no comment."** To viewers, "no comment" means "I'm guilty."

• **Establish the terms of a press interview before you say anything.** If you want to talk *off the record* or *on background only*, you must say so *before* you start talking. If you want to talk on the record but *not for attribution* (which means they can use the quote but not attribute it to you by name), you must say so *before* you start talking.

If you must go off the record or say something for non-attribution, try to limit it to one comment. Make clear when the quote starts and ends.

Going on and off the record too many times may confuse reporters who are trying to take notes. If that happens, it will increase the likelihood that something you didn't want to be quoted on will be used by mistake.

• **When talking on the record with a member of the press, don't talk about politics, money or polls.** Instead, talk about things voters are concerned about, like public policy matters.

• **Don't over-use press conferences.** Only use them when you need to make a major announcement and you want all the press there at the same time.

• **Make sure that your best, most colorful soundbite expresses precisely what you want to say.** That's because your best, most colorful soundbite – even if it's not the most important thing you say – is most likely to be what is used.

• **If during a taped interview, you flub up something, stop and ask the reporter for a chance to restate it correctly.** In most cases, they will be happy to comply.

• **If reporters "ambush" you unexpectedly, keep calm and take control.** Face them directly. Be friendly, cooperative. You don't want to look like a criminal being chased through the courthouse parking lot.

In such a situation, collect your thoughts, then determine what will be your major theme, your quotable soundbites. Try to steer the discussion to what *you* want to talk about.

Address one reporter at a time. Don't let them throw you off stride by yelling questions all at the same time. When answering each question, look the reporter straight in the eye. Keep steady eye contact with one reporter at a time.

After you've said what you want to say, and there has been a fair chance for reporters to ask enough questions, feel free to cut it off, politely and firmly.

The key is to look like you're in command, not in morbid fear. Never let them see you sweat.

Running Rich

With so many well-heeled people running for office these days, here are a few handy tips for wealthy candidates who finance their own campaigns. These suggestions should be kept in mind not only if you're a wealthy candidate but if you're running against one.

• **Position yourself as a populist advocate of average people and the powerless.** And don't just do it as a public relations gesture, internalize it and honestly believe in what you're doing. Whether you're a Republican or a Democrat, a liberal or a conservative, this is a vital inoculation strategy against eventual charges that you're an out-of-touch swell.

• **It's better to run as a civic leader than as a business person.** Many self-made candidates trumpet their business success and inadvertently appear smug in the process. Before you start your campaign, develop legitimate credentials as a tireless, selfless volunteer for community projects, charitable causes and nonpartisan public initiatives. That means more than just writing checks or going to glitzy fundraisers.

• **Don't spend all your money on TV ads.** The tube may be the single most powerful tool of mass communication, but don't forget the grassroots. Invest in field organization, direct mail and phones. Get average people to display your signs and stickers, and run local radio and newspaper ads to reinforce your people-to-people approach.

• **Don't spend all your time in TV studios, fancy restaurants or on the phone with big shots.** Go to bus stops and plant gates, shopping malls and hospitals, church picnics and schools. Shake hands, listen, relate. Forget what the deodorant commercials say; in this case, you want to let them see you sweat.

• **Avoid policy proposals that seem to serve your own financial interests.** Talk about issues that help people who make less in a year than you make in a day or a week. Be particularly careful about tax and fiscal policies that could be construed as being against the little guy.

If you don't believe me, ask Steve Forbes, the wealthy publisher. When he ran for the Republican presidenial nomination in 1996 on the "flat tax" issue, he demonstrated boldness and creativity; but the fact that his proposal would have saved very rich people – like himself – a lot of money damaged his credibility when speaking on the issue.

• **Don't boast about how much you're willing to spend on your campaign.** Voters want you to earn their votes, not buy them. They're also highly sensitive to a candidate's attitude and can detect "airs" a mile away. Don't apologize for your financial edge, but don't flaunt it either.

• **Remember the Nelson Rockefeller credo:** No matter what you do, you're going to take the hit for being rich, so you might as well get the benefit of a well-financed campaign.

Making the Right Appearance

• **Keep clean and look neat.** Candidates don't need to be beautiful or stylish to win elections, but they should present themselves properly. That means bathing regularly and making sure you never chance having body odor or bad breath.

Carry fresh clothes, deodorant, mouthwash, mints, dental floss, shaving supplies, cosmetics, tongue scrapers and a toothbrush in your car, and make frequent use of them just to be sure. John F. Kennedy was known to have changed shirts three or four times a day.

Also carry around pain killers (aspirin, Tylenol, etc.) and, if needed, antacid tablets. They may come in handy when you have a packed schedule but aren't feeling that great.

Male candidates should be careful shaving in the morning. Slow it down. Don't risk nicks and cuts that may bleed and scab.

• **Don't wear noticeably expensive jewelry unless it's a family heirloom with a good story behind it.** Good quality watches are acceptable, as long as they're not encrusted with tens of thousands of dollars worth of diamonds. Nice wedding rings are OK, even if they are expensive.

There's nothing wrong with candidates wearing nice things, but you don't want to be audaciously draped in valuable jewels and accessories. Coco Chanel always advised that after you get dressed, look at yourself in the mirror – then take one thing off. That's good advice for candidates.

• **If you need to lose weight, do it *before* you start**

campaigning. They say the TV camera puts 10 pounds on most people. So if you think you're too heavy in real life, think about those extra 10 pounds concentrated on your face.

By the way, most candidates lose 10-20 pounds during a hard campaign. If nothing else, running for office can be an effective weight reduction program. However, some candidates gain weight in campaigns because their diets are terrible and they nervously snack on a lot of high calorie, fatty junk foods.

• **Candidates should wash their hands after meeting and greeting lots of people.** You don't want to carry unnecessary germs.

• **Don't wear your own campaign lapel buttons and body stickers.** It looks tacky.

• **Get enough rest.** Candidates need to be in top form all the time. They need to think straight and look good. Don't let your staff push you beyond your limits. The major exception would be the last day or two before the election, when everybody's moving at full force, often around the clock.

• **About 10 minutes before you're introduced as the guest speaker at a banquet, excuse yourself and go to the restroom.** Take a hard look at yourself in the mirror, head to toe, including teeth, hair and clothes. Make sure everything is the way it's supposed to be.

• **Before you get up to deliver a speech, make sure there is a glass of water nearby.** You may need it to clear your throat at some point.

• **When speaking into a microphone at a podium, point it at your chin and not at your mouth.** This will help keep the sound from making a popping noise.

• **Never wear sunglasses when campaigning.** People like to look into your eyes.

Once when I was a state legislator, I got to a bridge dedication a minute or so after most of the other people had already taken their seats. It was a hot summer day and I had on my shades. As I strolled up the steps toward my seat, the master of ceremonies saw me and remarked, "And from Hollywood, here comes Ron Faucheux." Everybody laughed.

• **Wear clothes that look professional.** Be yourself. But don't dress too far down in an attempt to look like "one of the people." On the other hand, don't put on airs in an attempt to look important.

Lillian Brown, a noted image-consultant who has worked with scores of presidents, members of Congress, corporate CEOs and national news anchors, advises that candidates "need a few good, plain garments that can go anywhere, any time and adapt to many situations." She suggests, "good fabrics, perfect fit and classic look."

Good colors for most women, she says, are variations of light and dark blue, grey, burgundy, teal, purple, rust, taupe and olive green.

Brown recommends that candidates avoid black (unless you want to look older) and white (it glares, and adds weight).

Men should avoid wearing shiny fabrics. They should also stay away from loafers, except in casual settings. Lace-up shoes (black, preferably) look more substantial. Also, pull your socks up; bare shins are not becoming.

Women should avoid bare arms and spike heels. An unbroken line, with the same color from head to toe, is best for clothing. Women candidates should also invest in all-purpose blouses that can take them from morning to evening.

• **Wear makeup when you tape TV ads or do important TV interviews.** Please, have a professional apply it. For men, it's essential to cover a heavy beard, circles under the eyes, a shiny forehead and nose. Women generally need to use soft makeup to enhance their natural looks without looking "madeup."

• **Candidates can keep their personal trademarks, provided they're not outlandish.** Former New York U.S. Rep. Bell Abzug was famous for her hats. Former Illinois Sen. Paul Simon and Washington, D.C., Mayor Anthony Williams established identities with bow ties. A former governor of Wisconsin, Lee Dreyfus, always wore a red vest. Presidential candidate Al Smith was known for his brown derby in 1928. If you have such a trademark, and it fits your personality, keep it. But make sure it's not over-the-top or foolish looking.

Sometimes, candidates have created trademarks with a strategic purpose. Franklin Roosevelt wore distinctive pince nez eyeglasses and a crumbled hat with brim up in front. Those props, together with his wide smile and long cigarette holder clenched in his teeth, were used to draw attention *neck up*. Because of his polio, he wanted to focus the public eye toward his head and upper torso, diverting attention from the withered legs and heavy iron braces below.

There was the story of an old sheriff in South Louisiana who was running for re-election at the advent of the television age. The sheriff was known for always wearing dark glasses and a straw hat. When he showed up to do his first TV spot, his media consultant told him to take off the glasses and the hat. The old man protested, saying they were his trademarks. The media consultant insisted, explaining that a hat and dark glasses look silly on TV. So the sheriff took them off. But he looked so bad without them, the consultant told him to put them back on.

It just goes to show you: There's an exception to every rule in politics.

Appendix A

Sample Volunteer Card for Candidate and Personal Assistant to Carry

Smith for Mayor Volunteer Card

Your name_____

Address_____

City_____State_____Zip_____

Home Phone (_____)_____

Office Phone (_____)_____

Fax Number (_____)_____

E-mail_____

Your previous experience in political campaigns:

Yes, I'd like to:

❑ Work in headquarters   ❑ Contribute money

❑ Canvass my neighborhood   ❑ Put on a fundraiser

❑ Make phone calls   ❑ Put on a party/coffee/reception

❑ Send out postcards to friends & family ❑ Sell fundraising event tickets

❑ Other_____ *Thanks!*

Appendix B

Sample Candidate Scheduling Format

Meeting/Event Schedule Information

Date: July 19
Time You Must Be There: 8:20 p.m.
Time You Should Leave: 9:50-10:00 p.m.
Event: Ashton Chamber of
                                        Commerce Annual
Meeting
Location: Marriott Hotel, 1234 Airline
                                        Highway, Grand Ballroom
                                        on first floor near lobby
On-Site Contact: Jane Jones, cell 234-1234
Number of People Expected: 90-95
Schedule of Events:

Cocktail reception begins at 8:00 p.m.
Dinner starts at 8:30 p.m.
Your speech should begin at about 9:10 p.m.
You should finish your speech by about 9:30 p.m.
Stay and mingle after your speech for a little while.

What's Expected of You:

They want you to make a 20-minute speech on why you're running. They particularly want to hear your plans for small business, economic development and the landfill issue. There will be a short Q&A session after the speech. No other candidate will be there.

Who Will be There:

Fred Jones will introduce you around. Bobby and Barbara Phillips will also be there to introduce you to friends.

Materials to be Distributed:

George will bring 100 handcards that will be put on chairs. Will put stickers on table by door.

Directions:

Take I-66 west, exit 64, go left. One block, Marriott to the right. Park near main door. Fred and Bobby will meet you

Appendix C

Campaign Budget/Line-Item Work Sheet

Campaign Budget Work Sheet

$_____Television Ads
         time buys $_____
         production $_____

$_____Newspaper Ads
         space buys $_____
         production $_____

$_____Radio Ads
         time buys $_____
         production $_____

$_____Direct mail
(Do for each mail piece)
Mass mailings:
    printing $_____
    lists & labels $_____
    postage $_____
    mail shop $_____
    production & design $_____
Small in-house mailings
    printing $_____
    lists & labels $_____
    postage $_____
    mail shop $_____
    production & design $_____

$_____Polling and Research
    benchmark poll $_____
    follow-up polls $_____
    tracking polls $_____
    focus groups $_____
    issue research $_____
    opposition research $_____

$_____Outdoor Billboards
    space $_____
    production $_____

printing $_____

$_____**Printing and Materials**

brochures/fliers $_____

hand cards $_____

tabloids $_____

ballots $_____

letterhead & envelopes $_____

invitations $_____

yard signs $_____

posters $_____

bumper stickers $_____

body badges $_____

buttons $_____

design & layout $_____

$_____**Staff**

salaries $_____

expenses $_____

insurance $_____

taxes $_____

$_____**Headquarters**

rent $_____

office supplies $_____

equipment & furniture $_____

routine postage $_____

computer hardware $_____

software $_____

parking $_____

licenses & fees $_____

decorations $_____

petty cash $_____

refreshments/lunches/snacks $_____

broadcast fax services $_____

audio/video equipment $_____

$_____**Consultants**

General $_____

Media $_____

Other $_____

$_____Travel
             candidate & family $_____
             professional staff $_____
             volunteers $_____

$_____Legal & Accounting
    CPA/accounting/bookkeeping $_____
             Legal compliance $_____
             Qualifying/Filing fees $_____

$_____Telephone banks
             Leadership programs $_____
             Voter ID $_____
             Volunteer recruitment $_____
             Persuasion Calls $_____
             Defense Calls $_____
             GOTV $_____
             Other $_____

$_____Organizations
$_____Media training
$_____Photography
$_____Gifts and donations
$_____Voter registration programs
$_____Special absentee voting programs
             (in addition to above categories)
$_____Election day efforts (in addition to
             above categories)
$_____Other:_____
$_____Contingency (add up to 10%)

$_____TOTAL CAMPAIGN BUDGET